THE WORLD SOCIAL FORUM
STRATEGIES OF RESISTANCE

THE WORLD SOCIAL FORUM
STATEGIES OF RESISTANCE

José Corrêa Leite

In collaboration with Carolina Gil

Translated by Traci Romine

HaymarketBooks
Chicago, Illinois

© 2003, 2005 José Corrêa Leite
Translation © 2005 Traci Romine
All rights reserved. Published 2005 by Haymarket Books
P.O. Box 160185, Chicago, IL 60618
www.haymarketbooks.org

Originally published as *Fórum Social Mundial: A história de uma invenção política*, Editora Fundação Perseu Abramo, São Paulo, Brazil

Cover design by Eric Ruder
Cover photo: March of the Landless Rural Workers' Movement (MST) in Brazil in October 1999 protesting the government's economic polices and the International Monetary Fund (Photo: Antonio Scorza/AFP).

ISBN-10 : 1-931859-159
ISBN-13 : 978-1-931859-15-8

10 9 8 7 6 5 4 3 2 1
Printed in Canada.

Library of Congress Cataloging-in-Publication Data
Leite, José Corrêa.
  [Fórum Social Mundial. English]
  World Social Forum : strategies of resistance / José Corrêa Leite in collaboration with Carolina Gil ; translated by Traci Romine.
    p. cm.
Translation of: Fórum Social Mundial: a história de uma invenção política.
  Includes bibliographical references and index.
  ISBN 1-931859-15-9 (pbk.)
  1. World Social Forum 2. Anti-globalization movement. I. Gil, Carolina. II. Title.
  HN17.5.L443 2005
  303.48'4–dc22   2004026674

CONTENTS

9 World Social Forum Charter of Principles

15 Introduction

CHAPTER ONE
21 The Spirit of Seattle: The Neoliberal World Meets Its Specter

CHAPTER TWO
55 From Seattle to Genoa: The Protest Cycle

CHAPTER THREE
77 The World Social Forum: A Political Invention

CHAPTER FOUR
103 The Forum as a Global Movement Convergence Space

CHAPTER FIVE
123 Globalization and the Future of the World Social Forum

EPILOGUE
145 New Directions for the World Social Forum

165 "A Fête for the End of the End of History" by Naomi Klein

181 Calls to Action

209 Organizations

230 Chronology

241 Bibliography

256 Index

*To the brothers and sisters
of the
World Social Forum Secretariat*

World Social Forum Charter of Principles

The committee of Brazilian organizations that conceived of and organized the first World Social Forum, held in Porto Alegre from January 25 to 30, 2001, after evaluating the results of that Forum and the expectations it raised, considers it necessary and legitimate to draw up a Charter of Principles to guide the continued pursuit of that initiative. While the principles contained in this Charter—to be respected by all those who wish to take part in the process and to organize new editions of the World Social Forum—are a consolidation of the decisions that presided over the holding of the Porto Alegre Forum and ensured its success, they extend the reach of those decisions and define orientations that flow from their logic.

1. The World Social Forum is an open meeting place for reflective thinking, democratic debate of ideas, formulation of proposals, free exchange of experiences, and interlinking for effective action by groups and movements of civil society that are opposed to neoliberalism and to domination of the world by capital and any form of imperialism and are committed to building a planetary society directed toward fruitful relationships

among humankind and between it and the Earth.

2. The World Social Forum at Porto Alegre was an event localized in time and place. From now on, in the certainty proclaimed at Porto Alegre that "another world is possible," it becomes a permanent process of seeking and building alternatives, which cannot be reduced to the events supporting it.

3. The World Social Forum is a world process. All the meetings that are held as part of this process have an international dimension.

4. The alternatives proposed at the World Social Forum stand in opposition to a process of globalization commanded by the large multinational corporations and by the governments and international institutions at the service of those corporations' interests, with the complicity of national governments. They are designed to ensure that globalization in solidarity will prevail as a new stage in world history. This will respect universal human rights and those of all citizens—men and women—of all nations and the environment and will rest on democratic international systems and institutions at the service of social justice, equality, and the sovereignty of peoples.

5. The World Social Forum brings together and interlinks only organizations and movements of civil society from all the countries in the world but does not intend to be a body representing world civil society.

6. The meetings of the World Social Forum do not deliberate on behalf of the World Social Forum as a body. No one, therefore, will be authorized, on behalf of any of the editions of the Forum, to express positions claiming to be those of all its participants. The participants in the Forum shall not be called on to make decisions as a body, whether by vote or acclamation, on declarations or proposals for action that would commit all or the majority of them and that propose to be taken as es-

tablishing positions of the Forum as a body. It thus does not constitute a locus of power to be disputed by the participants in its meetings, nor does it intend to constitute the only option for interrelation and action by the organizations and movements that participate in it.

7. Nonetheless, organizations or groups of organizations that participate in the Forum meetings must be assured the right, during such meetings, to deliberate on declarations or actions they may decide on, whether singly or in coordination with other participants. The World Social Forum undertakes to circulate such decisions widely by the means at its disposal, without directing, hierarchizing, censuring, or restricting them, but as deliberations of the organizations or groups of organizations that made the decisions.

8. The World Social Forum is a plural, diversified, nonconfessional, nongovernmental, and nonparty context that, in a decentralized fashion, interrelates organizations and movements engaged in concrete action at levels from the local to the international to build another world.

9. The World Social Forum will always be a forum open to pluralism and to the diversity of activities and ways of engaging of the organizations and movements that decide to participate in it, as well as the diversity of genders, ethnicities, cultures, generations, and physical capacities, providing they abide by this Charter of Principles. Neither party representations nor military organizations shall participate in the Forum. Government leaders and members of legislatures who accept the commitments of this Charter may be invited to participate in a personal capacity.

10. The World Social Forum is opposed to all totalitarian and reductionist views of economy, development, and history and to the use of violence as a means of social control by the state. It upholds respect for human rights and the practices of

real democracy, participatory democracy, and peaceful relations in equality and solidarity among ethnicities, genders, and peoples; and condemns all forms of domination and subjection of one person by another.

11. As a forum for debate, the World Social Forum is a movement of ideas that prompts reflection, and the transparent circulation of the results of that reflection, on the mechanisms and instruments of domination by capital, on means and actions to resist and overcome that domination, and on the alternatives proposed to solve the problems of exclusion and social inequality that the process of capitalist globalization with its racist, sexist, and environmentally destructive dimensions is creating internationally and within countries.

12. As a framework for the exchange of experiences, the World Social Forum encourages understanding and mutual recognition among its participant organizations and movements, and places special value on the exchange among them, particularly on all that society is building to center economic activity and political action on meeting the needs of people and respecting nature, in the present and for future generations.

13. As a context for interrelations, the World Social Forum seeks to strengthen and create new national and international links among organizations and movements of society that—in both public and private life—will increase the capacity for nonviolent social resistance to the process of dehumanization the world is undergoing and to the violence used by the state, and reinforce the humanizing measures being taken by the action of these movements and organizations.

14. The World Social Forum is a process that encourages its participant organizations and movements to situate their actions, from the local level to the national level and seeking active participation in international contexts, as issues of planetary citi-

zenship, and to introduce onto the global agenda the change-inducing practices that they are experimenting in building a new world in solidarity.

Approved and adopted in São Paulo, Brazil, on April 9, 2001, by the organizations that make up the World Social Forum Organizing Committee, approved with modifications by the World Social Forum International Council on June 10, 2001.

Introduction

Beneath the rubble of the Berlin Wall and the Soviet Union rests, it is said, a story of utopias, regulated work, and national states. Capitalism, becoming irresistible and guaranteeing humanity a radiant future, had triumphed over socialism. The promise that everyone would finally become integrated into consumer society and prosper under liberal democracy in a peaceful world was echoed throughout the ever-present media. This conventional wisdom seemed to invade every pore of society, dominating all institutions, excluding any alternative. The Left, as it was organized in the twentieth century, would become an outdated force, marginalized in world politics. The only survivors would be those who "modernized" and began to accept the dominance of the market as the natural order for humanity.

Thanks to the civilizing force of capitalist globalization, humanity would finally transcend its particularities and become integrated into a planetary mercantile society. Fueled by technological progress, exemplified in the communications revolution, globalization would produce an information society, which would itself decipher, as with genomes, the code of life. Based upon a "new economy," this society would enable capitalism to escape its crises and cycles of recession.

As the market dictated, neoliberal policies—which have been common since 1979–80, when they were introduced by the governments of Ronald Reagan in the United States and Margaret Thatcher in England—were presented as the only viable model to enable progress. Open markets and economic liberalization, deregulation and reduced state intervention in the economy, privatization, intellectual property guarantees, reduced social spending, and increased global competition became incontestable commandments, sanctioned by the International Monetary Fund (IMF), the World Bank, the World Trade Organization (WTO), the G-8, and the European Union (EU). Challenges to this model were punished by capital flight and speculative attacks on national currencies.

Some recalcitrant voices still rose up against globalization and neoliberal economic science, such as the Zapatistas and French public-service strikers. Others tried to influence decision making in international organizations. But these were isolated dissonances in an enormous choir tuned to the idea of globalization ("globalitary," as Brazilian intellectual Milton Santos[*] would say), an idea that reigned unchallenged until the end of the 1990s.

Then, a new actor with the strength and appeal necessary

---

[*] The works of Milton Santos (1926–2001) are not widely translated into English. He coined this term, "globalitary," translated literally here, in his book *Por Outra Globalização* (For Another Globalization). Santos was a Brazilian geologist and intellectual who wrote more than forty books during his lifetime.

to reverse the political situation entered the scene. On November 30, 1999, in Seattle, Washington, fifty thousand demonstrators succeeded in blockading the ministerial meeting of the WTO. The meeting was suspended, and the opening of a new round of world trade negotiations was delayed. The failure of the WTO meeting was the result not only of public protests but also of conflicts of interest between key countries. Times were changing. Over the next two years, by the G-8 meeting in Genoa in July 2001, this new movement would organize huge mobilizations and protests at every important meeting of multilateral organizations that promoted the domination of the market over all social affairs.

For years, a global justice movement had been developing in different countries. Made up by a variety of organizations and networks, it fought against what in English-speaking countries is called "corporate globalization." Against government and business forces that pushed to subordinate everything to the market, a movement of movements—asserting that "the world is not a market" and "our world is not for sale"—came together. Neoliberal globalization had finally met the specter—pejoratively called the "antiglobalization" movement by its propaganda—capable of haunting it.

However, the global movement, a movement of movements, did not clash only with neoliberal globalization, which was hard-hit after 2000 by a recession that burst the "speculative bubble" of the 1990s and the mirage of the "new economy." It soon faced the unilateral, bellicose, and neocolonial shift that George W. Bush and his allies imposed on world politics, particularly after September 11, 2001. The new internationalism of the global justice movement transformed itself into a movement against war and empire. This antiwar movement grew rapidly between the wars in Afghanistan (2001) and Iraq (begun in 2003) and seems likely to become a permanent dimension of world politics. The project of combating neoliberal globalization and the militarization of international relations puts a more political stamp on the global movement, as the enormous worldwide antiwar protest marches showed on February 15, 2003. The movement began to be viewed as "another superpower," the only one capable of confronting the North American empire.

One of the great political innovations in this new movement is the World Social Forum, the place where, since January 2001, a large part of the global movement has met to debate and discuss its struggle. The World Social Forum sustains a new form of politics, a space that uses as its model the idea of horizontally structured networks, rather than a hierarchical pyramid. This model reduces points of dispute and facilitates the dynamic of dialogue and collaboration. The World Social Forum is an open space in which participants organize their own activities. It is not an organization or an institution. Political parties are removed from center stage, becoming supporting actors, and no final assembly or resolution assumes to speak for all of the participants. Diversity is thus respected and valued as a strength rather than a weakness of the movement. If "another world is possible," it will be a "world in which many worlds fit."

The World Social Forum sponsors a succession of events, forming a global process and leaving an indelible mark on participants. At these events, hundreds of thousands of activists from around the world meet in an environment of dialogue and collaboration. They are connecting to resistance, constructing alternatives to neoliberalism, and taking the lead in the organization of the twenty-first-century Left.

It is this invention and the deepening of this new form of political action that we will examine. In this text, I recount much of the collective work of the World Social Forum Secretariat. Naturally, however, the responsibility for the interpretation presented here is mine alone.

São Paulo, July 15, 2003

CHAPTER ONE

The Spirit of Seattle: The Neoliberal World Meets Its Specter

From what historical soil did the global movement and World Social Forum grow? We must answer this question in order to diagnose the present and to debate to what measure the current world is both a rupture with and a continuation of the past. Among analysts, there is rough agreement about the general lines of the story. The framework for understanding can be traced on two levels. On the one hand, there exist the great ages in the evolution of capitalism. If the capitalism of the nineteenth century was characterized by liberalism, by a competitive economy under the hegemony of the English empire, the dawning of the twentieth century saw a growth in protectionism and ever-greater interimperial conflicts, which produced the two great wars. On this terrain, neoliberal globalization, developing since 1980, represents a third great moment, a return to the trend toward the globalization of capital that was interrupted in the twentieth century by the crystallization of national economies that were able to protect themselves from world market pressure. Paulo Nogueira Batista Jr.

correctly characterized neoliberalism as "a revolt against the twentieth century." Capital escaped political-social controls that had been imposed and again received broad freedom for circulation and investment—mobility that did not reach the workforce, whose freedom to migrate is more greatly reduced than it was in the nineteenth century. Although they disagree on some specifics, many analysts accept the utility of the descriptive terms "competitive capitalism," "imperialistic capitalism," and "late capitalism" to designate the three different moments of world economic evolution in the last two centuries.

On the other hand, agreement on the historical panorama can be deepened by a political understanding of the twentieth century. English historian Eric Hobsbawm summarized it well in establishing the time period that he called the "Short Twentieth Century." This period begins in 1914 with the eruption of the First World War and closes in 1991 with the collapse of the Soviet Union. For Hobsbawm, the first part of this period is the "Age of Catastrophe" (1914–47), from the beginning of the First World War to the end of the Second World War. The second is the "Golden Age" (1947–73), when capitalism experienced its greatest prosperity in history. The final period, beginning in the mid-1970s, is the "Crisis Decades," which have continued beyond 1991. If the collapse of the Soviet Union represents the end of a great political period within which the twentieth century moved and, in this sense, the end of an historical epoch, the decades of crisis open a transition for the world in which we live, whose contours are still being established.

The changes under way become more evident when compared with the earlier period after the Second World War, a period of economic expansion in all corners of the planet, of welfare states in the developed countries and development in peripheral nations, of planned economies seeking to industrialize societies that had broken with capitalism. As such, global market structuring was undertaken within national economies that had a certain level of autonomy, in a bipolar world, with the United States and the Soviet Union at the center of international politics, and the decolonialization of European empires. It depended on capitalism based on Keynesian anticyclical political economics (state intervention, search for full employment, expansion of social rights, etc.) and on Fordist mass production schemes (assembly lines, huge factory units, expansion of the industrial working class). In this world flourished the social-democratic left and communists, the national liberation movement, and the left political culture focused on the historical role of the proletariat and the idea of revolution as a conquest of political power in the national state.

But while the "Golden Age" progressed, new social rights were conquered and capitalism, based on Keynesian-Fordist policies, forgot the past catastrophic crises; profit rates in the central countries began generally to fall and to affect countries' growth rates. Profit rates gradually fell, according to the Organization for Economic Co-operation and Development (OECD), from 22.5 percent in 1966 to 14.3 percent in 1982. Beginning in 1973, recessions—alleviated by anticyclical action in national governments in the postwar era—returned, without growth in public expenditures to offset them.

The response to lower profits became clear during the recession of 1980–82. Financial deregulation, opening of national economies, and privatization were conducted under the neoliberal policies of the Reagan and Thatcher governments and soon became the model for all developed countries' governments. This capitalist restructuring gained strength and promoted a vast rearrangement of class relations, reducing the influence of the working class and putting the industrial bourgeoisie of developing countries under pressure. It made possible and was accelerated by the new wave of internationalization of capital, above all, the internationalization of financial capital.

These changes rearrange power relations in favor of the most dynamic and strongest capitalist sectors that operate on a world scale to the detriment of all those that compete against them. The 1980s saw more pressure mounting against the bureaucratic societies allied with the Soviet Union and an exhaustion of anti-imperialist struggles in the developing countries (an ebbing of the Central American revolutions and struggles in Asia) and of workers' struggles in the central countries. Workers remained mobilized in the 1980s only in newly industrialized countries, such as Brazil, South Korea, and South Africa.

Neoliberalism gained new life at the dawn of the 1990s with the fall of the Berlin Wall and the collapse of the Soviet Union, which made the shift in the worldwide balance of class forces overwhelming and had short-term catastrophic political and ideological consequences for a large part of the Left. The world system of states that had underpinned twentieth-century international relationships, stabilized by the bipolarity imposed at the end of the Second World War, no longer existed. The world formed under the impact of the 1917 Russian Revolution also disappeared: the Union of Socialist Soviet Republics (USSR) was gone. Vanished also was the world divided between two superpowers, the national liberation movements that grew up within this framework, and the socialist movement dominated by two currents that fed each other (social democrats and communists). As Daniel Bensaïd reminds us, we watched in Europe alone the formation of seventeen new countries and 14,000 kilometers of new borders in the first half of the 1990s.

NEOLIBERAL GLOBALIZATION: A NEW PHASE OF CAPITALISM

The most outstanding evidence for the passage of the historical epoch is globalization, a new wave of internationalization of capital. After almost a century of protectionism and economic structuring based fundamentally on national dynamics, we return to a new period in which internationalized financial capital predominates, as Paul Hirst and Grahame Thompson remind us well in drawing an analogy to British hegemony of the nineteenth century. As it was then, today's neoliberalism and globalization are leading the conscious effort of imperial power to reconquer North American hegemony (the "strong-dollar diplomacy") and are, from their inception, part of the construction of what José Luis Fiori called a new "imperial system." Capitalist globalization, strongly supported by the governments of the world's most powerful countries, begins with forcing national markets to open (which Brazil experienced under Fernando Collar in 1990) and to deregulate, as well as with huge multinational corporations purchasing small companies, earlier protected in their countries, by the privatization of public companies, and then with the crisis of Keynesian economic political instruments, undermined by public debt and lowering the tax burden on the rich.

The rearrangement of social and political power relations unleashes a series of processes that feed this dynamic: corporate mergers, accelerating the centralization and concentration of capital on a world scale; the reduction of capital replacement cycles (by means of investments with shorter returns), which enables an increase in profit rates; investment diversification by large corporations, which also move into finance, integrating in the "casino economy"; changes in work

---

International Monetary Fund

With the goal of world economic reconstruction after the Second World War, three international institutions were proposed in 1944: the International Monetary Fund (IMF), the World Bank, and the International Trade Organization (ITO). When the war ended in 1945, the IMF and the World Bank were established, but the ITO was not. It was created in 1995 under the name World Trade Organization (WTO).

The IMF was established in July 1944, when the Final Articles of Agreement of the United Nations International Monetary and Financial Conference in Bretton Woods, New Hampshire, was signed, marking it as one of the first treaties to cover economy and finance.

The organization's primary arena is the international monetary system; it promotes equilibrium of the balance of payments as the best way to stabilize a country's economy. Its creation was based upon the assumption of free circulation of goods

organization, which produce a drop in the percentage of full-time, salaried workers as a total of the working class and an increase in the numbers of part-time, contingent, and informal-sector workers; a substitution of full employment by growing structural unemployment and by attacks on social security systems.

Profit rates rose gradually, but economic growth rates in central countries continued to decline, and the process was punctuated by global recessions (1974–75, 1980–82, 1990–92, 2001–02). In a world market composed of more open economies, competition becomes fiercer. Within this frame-

---

and capital between countries.

When it was formed, 29 countries made up the organization, but this number has grown to 184 member countries today. Beginning with the debt crises in the 1970s, developing countries began to join the IMF, which granted loans to nations that adopted "structural adjustment programs." Countries receive economic policy recommendations and are guaranteed transfers of resources, which today total around $300 billion. The IMF establishes guidelines that member countries must follow: international monetary cooperation, promotion of expansion and balanced growth of the financial system within the international scene, stabilization of the exchange rate, collaboration with the established multilateral payment system, determination of a gold-dollar standard, and the creation of a financial fund. This model also imposes privatization of state companies, economic stabilization, and government reform following neoliberal guidelines.

IMF resources are provided from a common fund, to which each country is obliged to subscribe when it enters the institu-

work, economic development is neither a probable nor a possible horizon for an immense number of poor countries. As Giovanni Arrighi points out, only a few countries, the strongest, can be winners in the race for the top spots in the world market.

The economic fundamentals of reorganizing class relations are achieved, above all else, through changes in management methods. "Lean production" is based on quality-control circles and teamwork, on one hand, and on flexibility, instability, intensified work rhythms, outsourcing, and reengineering—all of which are measures destined to raise the average exploitation

---

tion. In this manner, a general account is created, which is named Special Drawing Rights (SDR). All countries that make up the IMF contribute a determined quota established in accord with the financial situation of each country. Some norms were created in order to obtain an SDR loan. Among them, all loans must be limited to 60 percent of the total quota contributed by the country. If a country solicits less than 25 percent of its quota, it will not be obliged to set up a special program. If it exceeds this percentage, however, the country's government has to commit to take certain economic measures demanded by the IMF and expressed in its letter of intent.

The quota system conditions the voting power of each country within the IMF: each country has 250 votes and one additional vote per each $100,000 deposited in the general account. This unequal voting system gives members unequal power within the institution. Countries such as the United States that have a large number of votes are able to impose whatever decision they find convenient.

rate of workers—on the other. Structural unemployment, presented by neoliberalism as a necessary by-product of technical progress, is in fact a consequence of weaker economic growth rates overall and a small reduction in the average workweek.*

Institutions linked to globalization become ever more present and active, whether in the field of world trade (WTO), policy making (G-8), debt management (IMF-IBRD), or the environment (ECO-92, Kyoto Protocol). The conversion of the General Agreement on Tariffs and Trade (GATT) into the World Trade Organization (WTO) corresponds to the development of new methods of subordinating states, elected powers, and national legislatures to the global market. Under the aegis of the IMF and the World Bank, external debt acts to discipline dependent countries. These institutions, although weak compared to the core states and large corporations, are sufficiently powerful to constrain the countries of the Third World and Eastern Europe, which are moving toward capitalism.

But the trend toward globalization is, in part, counteracted by the formation of regional and continental blocs, through very different processes. These range from the European proto-state, which has many of the attributes earlier found in national states, to the North American Free Trade Agreement (NAFTA), which is just a commercial bloc centered around the United States, to Mercosur, whose destiny is still undetermined.

This is a scenario of upheaval and great instability, in which contradictory trends are at work in response to both "multilateral" and "neocolonial" pressures. When faced with

---
* This is perhaps a European-specific phenomenon. The more common U.S. pattern is increased hours worked for less pay.

the collapse (or "failure") of some states, international "stabilization" (or "humanitarian") interventions were assembled, in all cases at the initiative of the United States, with the support of multilateral organizations. Meanwhile, the logic of multilateral globalization tends to establish new norms of international law, as in the case of the International Court of Justice. But, following 2001, U.S. politics adopted a clear neocolonial and unilateralist character, provoking conflicts with U.S. allies in Europe.

Through these ongoing processes, market relations continue to penetrate all pores of society, subverting traditions, breaking community ties, destroying ancient collective identities, and promoting individualistic consumption. The expansion of the world market is the cause of deep changes in the social fabric, in a process in which, to paraphrase Marx, all that is solid melts into the air. It promotes a separation between the

World Bank

The International Bank of Reconstruction and Development (IBRD), better known as the World Bank, was created officially in 1945 as a United Nations specialized agency to reconstruct postwar Western Europe and Japan. In these countries, it financed infrastructure projects such as highways, railroads, and telecommunications. Since then, it has changed its methods in light of the changing world scene. Since the 1970s, the bank had focused its actions in developing countries, where it prioritized agricultural and educational programs, tying them to privatization and market competition. Currently, 184 countries are members of the bank.

economic and the political, as Bensaïd points out. The majority of national economies are no longer relatively coherent blocs, joining together market, territory, and state. International deregulation and competition introduce fractures between economic logic and political sovereignty. Inequality deepens between winners and losers in the race toward globalization on the international scale and between regions inside countries. With the reconcentration of power, a new hierarchy is established, but centered in world cities rather than countries. This growing inequality causes battles over fiscal resources, increasing regional disparities. Promises that underpinned the social welfare state are also questioned, producing social policies focused only on helping the poorest temporarily rather than providing services to all as a matter of right. The range of public health, welfare, and education services is reduced, and many services are privatized.

At the beginning of the 1990s, the World Bank focused on Eastern Europe, prioritizing environmental projects and financing farmers and businesspeople. Recently, the central concern has been the international financial crisis. In providing credit, the World Bank provides technical assistance to member countries, does research, and produces periodic reports showing how its resources should be used. In conjunction with the IMF, the World Bank applies economic adjustment programs in developing countries. The resources for IBRD's operations are generated by financial market transactions and by payments from countries that receive bank financing.

Social cohesion decreases as the state's role in the redistribution of wealth is reduced and state institutions lose legitimacy, overcome by the effects of privatization (reinforcing private economic power) and globalization (with the loss of control over economic and monetary relations). The restructuring of public debt, the shifting of the tax burden from the rich to the poor, and the crisis of public finances undermine the possibility of the welfare state (or a substitute for it) to preserve salaries, public services, and social protection. In dependent countries, this provokes a generalized crisis of public systems. In the worst cases, in which the local elite is unable to adjust to the

G-8: Group of the Rich

What is now the G-8 was created in 1975 with only six countries: the United States, France, Great Britain, Germany, Italy, and Japan. At the 1976 summit in San Juan, Puerto Rico, the group incorporated Canada and became known as the G-7, the group of the world's richest countries. Beginning in 1994, with the Naples summit, the G-7 began to meet with Russia and became known as the Political 8. At the summit in Birmingham, England, in 1998, Russia was brought into the group, which became the G-8, despite the fact that the G-7 continued to function as a unit. The entrance of the Russian Federation into the group was made possible through unprecedented concessions from Russia regarding the expansion of NATO into countries of the former Soviet Union.

The annual summits of chiefs of state and governments discuss macroeconomic management, international trade, and relations with developing countries. Other issues considered are

new reality, paternalistic distribution of benefits that leads to the heightening of tensions between clan/ethnic or religious groups occurs, particularly in Africa and Asia. In all cases, the legitimacy of political systems has been eroded, a trend manifested in abstention in national and local elections and a crisis of representation in leftist political parties, which see their historical justification for existence questioned.

Capitalist restructuring promotes large-scale restructuring of the working class. Participation of salaried workers in manufacturing declined until stabilizing in the 1990s at around 20 percent of the workforce in central countries (or less in the >

---

economic relations between the West and the East, energy, terrorism, labor, information technologies, organized crime and drugs, human rights, and arms control. Its declared objective is to coordinate economic and monetary policy worldwide.

In addition to the annual summits, the G-7/G-8 also created ministerial meetings, which enable ministers, such as those of finance and environment, to pursue work agreed on at each summit. The summits intend to provide direction to the international community, stipulating priorities, defining new issues, and giving guidelines to international organizations. At the meeting in 1997 in Denver, Colorado, the divergences between the more protectionist European Union economic model and the North American model became apparent. The United States pressured the European governments for greater economic access for North American products and services to markets on the continent. Disagreement over environmental policies was also expressed, with the United States, Japan, and Canada resisting a European proposal for greenhouse gas emissions reductions. At the 2000 >

United States, where the decline of the manufacturing workforce started earlier). Women's participation in the workforce is growing, but in precarious or part-time jobs. The largest part of the working class is linked to the services sector; McDonald's today employs more people than the metal industry in the United States. Meanwhile, business initiatives aimed at increasing work productivity increase the social heterogeneity of salaried workers, eroding their earlier ties of identity and solidarity, making resistance to these measures more difficult. Nevertheless, globally considered, there is a huge quantitative rise in the proletariat, though its conditions are less stable than before. Accelerated and chaotic urbanization also promotes, across the planet, a growth in excluded masses in huge metropolises, principally on the system's periphery. International movements of populations return with the rise in national and continental disparities or the regression of peripheral economies. If earlier immigration flowed from Europe to America (or forced migration from Africa or Asia to America), it now flows from all from peripheral to central countries, frequently

---

summit in Okinawa, Japan, the members of the G-7 could not reach agreement on the creation of a coordinated exchange rate policy.

Liberalizing policies and environmental issues are some of the points of protest against the G-8, as well as its attempt to coordinate worldwide economic and monetary policy according to these countries' interests. Since the Birmingham summit in England, global movements have protested against its meetings and its decisions.

under illegal conditions and in a climate of crisis, with growing marginalization and xenophobia.

Globalization displays, however, some ability to build a new power network, involving rootless elites, hierarchically organized around the bourgeoisies of the rich countries. These elites in the poor countries are plugged into the global elite and share similar interests, lifestyles, and values, as well as, to a certain extent, a common culture, separating them from the masses of the society in which they live. What in the past represented the adoption of the colonial lifestyle by the colonized today is presented as the adherence to a planetary culture, which the media disseminate everywhere. This alters the form in which these sectors relate to the other social classes. If one part of the dominant class responds to the country's poor as new "dangerous classes," the other part is still attempting to become socially and culturally integrated. Acceptance and dissemination of multiculturalism responds, at least in part, to this objective, incorporating expressions of the nonhegemonic sector identities in the expanded circuits of industrial culture.

Ancestral and suppressed identities are born and reborn through religious fundamentalism and xenophobic nationalism, to the extent that class and national solidarity links are weakened. On the other hand, in a perverse cycle, resistance to the new market-dominated "globalitary" universalism can also feed racism and new forms of exclusion, as well as social and political violence. Responses of solidarity and common identification as "citizens" promoted by some political and social movements are not the dominant trend in the developing world.

Capitalist restructuring, as such, has a strong dimension of regressive economic, social, political, and cultural counter-reform. The marriage between the unbridled free market and parliamentary democracy is failing to live up to any of neoliberalism's promises.

VERTIGO, IDEOLOGICAL CRISIS, AND THE PERMANENCE OF UTOPIAN ASPIRATIONS

The destruction of reference points that formerly organized worldviews and political action is enormous. Capitalism presents itself as the unique civilization and neoliberalism as the only possible ideology. Different worldviews and political ideologies, which had coexisted, confronted, and complemented each other during the expansion of postwar capitalism, entered into crisis. The three great ideological postwar responses—productivist bureaucratic communism, Third World development, and socialist alternatives—collapsed at virtually the same time, as Samir Amin has pointed out, with the only, very uncharacteristic survivor a social democracy adhering, to different degrees, to liberalism. The idea of expanding social and political rights and visions of progress were diminished. The presence of organized capital in all spheres of activity subverts the coordinates that discipline time and space, consciousness and political action, producing a dizzying sensation of vertigo.

Globalization brings together societies that earlier appeared far from each other, a compression of space-time that speeds up the pace of change in economic and social relations, while a global media network saturates all populations with information and images. The content disseminated by the culture industry becomes more wide reaching, taking on a character ever more market-driven, with the standardization of dissemination of information and entertainment provided by a sector that is highly concentrated on a planetary scale. The Hollywood standard of entertainment is intimately connected to the diffusion of a lifestyle and consumption ideal. Cultural transformations occur in strict harmony with globalization, justifying it and frequently expressing its most regressive dimensions. The globalized media symbolically integrates the world, unraveling cultural borders. Cultural isolation is no longer possible, and fundamentalism is often a form of resistance and reaffirmation of identity, which is being undermined, thus giving rise to "culture wars" or "clashes of civilization" or even, more globally, to the perception (held by postmodernism) that transforming culture is the most important task facing society.

When the models for explaining reality no longer appear to explain the individual's place in society, a generalized sensation of fragmentation results. In this vacuum, neoliberal ideology thrives, building on hegemonic values and referencing dominant practices; legitimizing the growing inequality among individuals and social classes, regions, and countries; and seeking to remove the possibility of questioning the market. It rules out as unrealistic or totalitarian any notion of another society, promoting the ideal of a capitalism under which individuals can achieve happiness as consumers in the market—consumers of the twenty-first century and citizens of the eighteenth century, Néstor García Canclini would say.

There is a paradoxical multiplication and crisis of utopias. Utopian aspirations erupt everywhere, highlighting the material abundance achieved by humanity and the possibility of general well-being, the equality or equivalence of genders, the recognition of different cultures, the enjoyment of sexual diversity, the search for perfect health, total communication, or of a society reconciled with nature. Meanwhile, the desired society, which could effectively provide these objectives, seems more distant than ever. Utopian promises of socialism are discredited by the collapse of bureaucratic and despotic regimes; social-democratic projects have been drastically scaled back; the idea of revolution tends to disappear from the horizon. Even a nation loses its progressive content, according to the republican ideal. No longer presenting itself as a community based on fraternity among its members, it is transformed into a wellspring of exclusionary, xenophobic nationalism. Many analysts have highlighted these phenomena as manifestations of a form of modern barbarism, bringing enormous risks to humanity and continuing to grow, seemingly without any possibility of stopping them.

This has profound destabilizing effects, given that human emancipation—be it the "pursuit of happiness" or "liberty for all"—had been the most elevated goal to guide political action and the formation of political projects since the Enlightenment. The twentieth century pursued, in different ways, these emancipatory objectives: in its first half, through political revolution, which would open the transition to socialism and the earthly utopia of tomorrow; modernist culture, whose criticism of capitalist modernity was employed from a utopian horizon already achieved by humanity; and, in general, through the conquest of mass political democracy. When these utopian aspirations reemerged, principally in developed countries in the 1960s, they were so rich and multifaceted that they appeared to anticipate an enduring period in which all expressions of protest could be manifested and legitimized. As such, the fundamental experience that constitutes the existing past within left-wing politics presupposes a normative horizon of full human emancipation—until the experiences associated with these politics had been brutally shaken, over the past two decades, by a crisis of utopian aspiration that dislodged this horizon. At the same time, recent decades saw a radicalization of new social actors and movements. Women, people of color, indigenous people, homosexuals, oppressed nationalities, immigrants, students, youth, the elderly, ecological groups, cultural movements, landless and homeless populations, and many other sectors expressed their demands, autonomy, and identity. All over the planet, supporting each other as examples, they seek to affirm their aspirations. The term "social movements" attempts to account for these myriad characters, old and new.

At the same time, the two great actors around which politics had been organized since the nineteenth century retreated: on one hand, national movements and parties, which sought to embody a nation in a state, the state in a nation (in the case of Brazil), or to affirm it in the face of other nations; on the other hand, the socialist movement, which based itself on the organization of the working class. Globalization limited the room to maneuver for the majority of national states. The collapse of the bureaucratic system in the Soviet Union eliminated the counterweight against the United States and undermined another justification for the welfare state, which was seen as another limiter of capitalistic market action. No established political institution seems to have the ability to counter the structural forces of the world market, to check the imperial power of the United States and the great multinational corporations of various origins that move within its wake. Meanwhile, the socialist movement's crisis not only expresses the general shift in the balance of social forces but also is the result of the project put into practice in the twentieth century and of the constitutive discourse of its own movement. The social recomposition of the proletariat contributes to the weakening of the old class organization. Labor unions lose their position in the spotlight and tend to be viewed as one more social movement. Socialists encounter enormous difficulty everywhere in pursuing anticapitalist policies.

Finally, the globalized world is too remote to permit the full development of the individual as a political subject, defended by classic liberal utopia. The production of the individual, free of the ties that bound him or her to traditional collectives, is driven by the expansion of the market, which dissolves old communities and ties of solidarity. However, the new capitalism undermines preconditions of exercising citizenship as participation in a vigorous public sphere. Atomized individuals —unable in their day-to-day lives to forge collectives strong enough to guide central political institutions—are transformed into simple consumers, gears in the mechanisms of established power, imprisoned by processes that escape any kind of democratic control. The culture industry's captivation of the world increases this crisis of the free individual under the spell of liberalism. It reinforces what is characterized as the narcissistic (Christopher Lasch) or depressive (Elisabeth Roudinesco) personality.

In this manner, when almost all things appear possible and a multiplicity of political actors emerges, no strategy appears to work and no actor appears effective enough to question the fundamentals of the established social structure or to exercise real self-determination in the face of power. Today the multiplication and crisis of political actors are simultaneous. It is on this ground that the global movement emerges, and within it, the World Social Forum.

THE GLOBAL MOVEMENT'S ROOTS

As neoliberal policies became a coherent project during the 1980s, resistance rapidly emerged, but it was ruthlessly crushed. This was the case in the failure of the long miners' strike in England in 1984–85 and of the 1983–84 Italian workers' movement in defense of a *scala mobile* that tied wage increases to inflation. But neoliberalism took on the contours of a global policy only after 1992, with the United States exercising its hegemony through multilateral institutions in coordination with the other capitalist powers. In 1990, British prime minister Margaret Thatcher left power and Britain joined the European unification process, and in 1993, Bill Clinton replaced George Bush Sr. as president of the United States after twelve years of Republican rule. Multilateral institutions took over management of capitalist globalization for the second-generation neoliberal governments. The formation of the WTO in 1995 was an important step in this process, creating a central triad with the IMF and World Bank of world economic institutions. The WTO not only regulated the trade of merchandise but also incorporated a treaty on intellectual property, the TRIPS agreement (Trade-Related Aspects of Intellectual Property Rights), which lengthened the validation period of patents, restricted the production of medicines outside the control of large laboratories, and permitted gene patenting. The WTO was also given the responsibility to negotiate liberalization of services and a new agreement on agriculture. A trade dispute resolution panel was also established, with no rights of appeal. The constitution of the WTO was accompanied by other liberalizing initiatives: NAFTA between the United States, Canada, and Mexico, and the Maastricht Treaty, which set the European Union into a neoliberal mold (based on fiscal austerity criteria, a single currency, and a European Central Bank), both signed in 1993.

European Union

The European Union (EU) was established in 1992, with the signing of the Maastricht Treaty, replacing the European Economic Community (EEC) that had been established in 1957 by the Treaty of Rome. The embryo of the EEC was the European Coal and Steel Community, formed by Belgium, Germany, France, Italy, Luxembourg, and The Netherlands.

The Maastricht Treaty created a bloc, which expanded to twenty-five member states in 2004, to remove barriers to the circulation of goods, capital, services, and people. The integration was accomplished under a clear neoliberal orientation, which was intensified by the adoption of a single currency, the Euro. Meanwhile, the governments of France and Germany promoted a policy of strengthening supernational institutions, such as the European Council, the European Parliament, and the Central Bank, directed by bureaucrats and immune to any

The process of setting up these multilateral institutions was accompanied everywhere by offensives against social rights, on one hand, and by increased misery, inequality, and exclusion on the other. In response, new resistance, frequently with an innovative political character, emerged throughout the world.

Two initial resistance movements were particularly notable. The Zapatista Army of National Liberation (EZLN), from the Chiapas region, one of the poorest states in Mexico, launched an unexpected and spectacular popular insurrection on January 1, 1994, the day NAFTA took effect. The EZLN is a movement of indigenous people that draws inspiration from various sources, as Michael Löwy has shown: recapturing the

---

type of public control. A debate about a European Constitution is also under way, signaling a possible political unification.

In 1999, eleven countries adhered to the Euro (Greece was admitted into the "Euro zone" in 2001). At first, the single currency was adopted only as a reference unit in commercial and financial transactions. In January 2002, the printed Euro currency entered circulation. Only Denmark, the United Kingdom, and Sweden continued to maintain a national currency.

In conjunction with the process of strengthening the already existing EU, there is a process of expansion, which began in negotiations opened during the 1998 EU summit. The adhesion process is slow, however, because of the economic demands made on new members. The Central Bank of Europe demands balanced budgets, a deficit of not more than 3 percent of GDP, and indebtedness of less than 60 percent. In addition, inflation must be low and maintained in balance, and alterations of labor and social security legislation are demanded.

legacy of Che Guevara, the struggle of Emiliano Zapata, liberation theology, Mayan culture, and the democratic demands of Mexican society. Defending the idea that it is possible to change the world without taking power, the Zapatistas found an echo in many movements. In July and August 1996, they held the First Intercontinental Meeting for Humanity and Against Neoliberalism, which brought together four thousand participants in the Lacandona jungle in Chiapas.

The second important resistance movement was that of French government workers who paralyzed public services

Fourth Declaration of the Lacandon Jungle

Brothers and Sisters:

Many words walk in the world. Many worlds are made. Many worlds are made for us. There are words and worlds, which are lies and injustices. There are words and worlds which are truths and truthful. We make true worlds. We have been made from true words.

In the world of the powerful there is no space for anyone but themselves and their servants. In the world we want everyone fits. The world we want is one in which many worlds fit. The Nation we want to construct is one in which all communities and languages fit, where all steps may walk, where all may have laughter, where all may live the dawn.

We speak of unity even when we are silent. Softly and gently we speak the words that find the unity that will embrace us in history and will discard the abandonment, which confronts and destroys us.

Our word, our song and our cry, is so that the dead will no

in December 1995 with great popular support. This struggle again raised the discussion in Europe about the meaning of neoliberal policies, which were being applied unquestioningly. Other signs of a changing climate appeared in Asia as well, with the workers' strikes against private companies in South Korea in 1997, and even in the United States with the growing involvement of unions, students, and environmental groups in the fight against the consequences of NAFTA. These changes swept John Sweeney into the presidency of the AFL-CIO in October 1995 and sparked strikes, including

---

longer die. So that we may live, fighting: so that we may live, singing. Long live the word. Long live Enough is Enough! Long live the night, which creates the morning. Long live our dignified walk together with all those who cry. To destroy the death clock of the powerful, we fight. For a new lifetime, we fight.

The lower of the world is not dead, even in silence our steps walk. In silence our word is sown. For our cries to flourish, we remain silent. The word creates the soldier in order not to die in oblivion. In order to live, the word dies, its seed sown forever in the womb of the earth. By being born and living, we die. We will always live. We will not surrender. Only those who give up their history are consigned to oblivion. We are here. We do not surrender. Zapata is alive, and in spite of everything, the struggle continues.

From the mountains of Southeast Mexico
Insurgent Sub-commander Marcos
Indigenous Clandestine Revolutionary Committee
General Command of the Zapatista Army of National Liberation
Mexico, January 1996

those against UPS, General Motors, and Boeing.

The new and growing resistance emerged in the context of the maturation of great social change, produced around the world, by a long period of neoliberal globalization. First, past decades saw what David Harvey called a wave of "time-space compression," a series of complementary economic, social, and technological transformations that made the world smaller and more integrated, accelerating the circulation of capital, social relationships, contacts, and cultural changes. Information technology, the Internet, and media with global reach provided a technological foundation for a new leap in the internationalization of capital, new management methods and work organization, new cultural practices, and new means of comprehending the world. This is the social root of the media culture—fragmented, multicultural, individualist, consumerist, and disengaged—which is frequently labeled "postmodernism." Second, global problems and the perception of them by important layers of the population increased during this period. It began to be believed that many problems involving the environment, human rights, democracy, labor, cultural production, organized crime, control of financial markets and capital speculation, international trade, and development could only be confronted by international initiatives. These problems have their roots in the radical marketization of life in these decades, linked to the internationalization of capital, markets, and finance; the reduction of the relative weight of the majority of national states in social life; the unequal and unparalleled cultural interrelationship in consumer fashions and habits; and the uprooting of a technocratic, capitalist elite from its society. Coupled with time-space compression, this spurs new generations to fight against the symbols of globalized culture (e.g., McDonald's and Nike).

Third, the internationalization of campaigns and battles in response to these global changes increased sharply. United Nations thematic conferences since the 1980s have become ever larger targets for activists and members of nongovernmental organizations (NGOs), but ECO-92 (the 1992 Earth Summit) in Brazil symbolized a qualitative shift in the growing mobilization of worldwide civil society. World Bank meetings were followed not only by NGOs and lobbyists but also by protests involving groups radically opposed to World Bank policies. Demonstrations accompanied G-7 meetings. Entities such as Greenpeace and Amnesty International, which had been acting often against these targets, established battlefield coordinates on an international terrain. And activists started to protest companies such as Monsanto, McDonald's, Exxon, and Nike, establishing an important network of organizations that today monitors these companies' activities.

Fourth, a new radicalization gradually took shape among young people, mainly in central capitalist countries but also in the periphery. After decades of apathy, fragmentation, and consumerism, a new left political generation emerged, the first since 1968. However, after such a long period of political paralysis and reaction, it blossomed largely beyond and against the established political organizations and reference points.

The student movement, in solidarity with workers and those involved in environmental causes, grew rapidly in the United States in the 1990s, principally in the fight against sweatshops (textile industries that make clothing in unsafe working conditions and frequently employ illegal immigrant workers). This led a section of young people to perceive that multinational corporations and the international organisms they control were responsible for great tragedies. In Europe and North America, direct-action movements have grown for many years—vaguely inspired by the Situationist International of the 1960s (referenced in Guy Debord's work), anarchism, and autonomism. Since 1995, the English group Reclaim the Streets, which promoted street parties and other types of civil disobedience, organized anticapitalist mobilizations, culminating in the gigantic invasion of London's banking district in June 1999. In Italy, the social centers movement sustained the Tutte Bianchi or Disobbedienti, which played a prominent role in all of the European protests. Youth activism also spread through the developing countries—in Mexico City, a huge strike at National Autonomous University of Mexico (UNAM) in 1999; in Seoul, in alliance with KCTU unionists; and in Buenos Aires, in massive blockades by protesters (*piqueteros* in Spanish).

Young people gave the global movement much of its dynamism and, in many countries, helped to stimulate activism among older militant sectors and partnerships with social movements. The radicalization of youth almost always heralds more profound change: young people do not bear the weight of losses suffered by earlier generations. Instead their own experiences push them to act. In addition, an ever widening historical gap separates them from the political end of the twentieth century, brought to a close in 1989–91. This is an existential fact that would become the backbone of the movement, composed of people generally in their twenties, that gained force in Seattle. They grew up listening to the promises of neoliberalism and became frustrated by living through the concrete consequences of the marketization of the land, water, air, education, and life. The resurgence of anticapitalism appears, as such, to be part of a more general distrust in the system, its institutions, and established political practices, including those of the traditional Left, which has been integrated into the system. Mass mobilizations, direct action, and civil disobedience appear as logical paths of protest and the fight for alternatives, increasing the distance between the Left forged before the 1990s and the one developing today.

Finally, the ideological and political prisms through which those opposed to neoliberal globalization understood themselves and voiced their concerns changed significantly. During the second half of the 1990s, a whole series of social movements, NGOs, and leftist sectors were already critically debating globalization, which was very different from what had existed up to that point. The notion of living in a new historical epoch came from two sources: on the one hand, from those who had already identified the transformations under way in capitalism, such as David Harvey and Fredric Jameson, and on the other, by those who debated the historical significance of the Soviet Union's collapse (the work that had the most impact on the Left was, certainly, *The Age of Extremes* by Eric Hobsbawm, published in 1994). This conviction that they were living in a new epoch opened space for a series of critical and self-critical reflections about the visions and strategies so focused on national terrain in the earlier period; the simultaneous crises of the national liberation movements, bureaucratic communism, and social-democratic reformism now fed a new type of international theorizing. The scenario in which revolution was no longer (at least for a while) the order of the day, as vehemently expressed by the Zapatistas, would also open new paths of political experimentation. As such, the strong criticisms of neoliberalism offered opportunities as much to voices active since the 1960s and 1970s—such as Noam Chomsky, Susan George, and Toni Negri—who now found a reinvigorated audience, as they did to others who became prominent in the 1990s and who, like Naomi Klein, were only a few years older than the average protester. A new agenda was being constructed not only of political initiatives but also of theoretical formulations by people such as Filipino activist Walden Bello and English journalist George Monbiot, and in the radical political engagement of Pierre Bourdieu and other authors who linked their ideas to the pages of *Le Monde Diplomatique*.

The emergence of a grave financial crisis in Asia in the second half of 1997, which spread in 1998 to Russia and Brazil, revealed to an important part of the world the limits of the prosperity that neoliberal propaganda promised. At the same time, the first drafts of the Multilateral Agreement on Investment (MAI) began to emerge, setting off alarms among those already cognizant of neoliberalism's adverse consequences. This provoked new mobilizations. The instability and fragility of the neoliberal model became evident, as did the poor countries' failure to partake in the "irrational exuberance of the market," as Alan Greenspan called the speculative bubble that lasted until 2000 in North American stock exchanges. Consciousness of neoliberalism's failure as a development strategy and the devastating impacts of market anarchy were increasingly obvious. The legitimacy of the neoliberal ideology of globalization was beginning to be questioned.

Resistance began to accelerate in 1997. Between April and June of that year, we had the first European march against unemployment and exclusion, which ended with a demonstration of fifty thousand people in June in Amsterdam, Holland, on the occasion of the European Summit. In May, the Continental Social Alliance (CSA) was formed during the Third Union Summit meeting, held in conjunction with the ministerial meeting of the Free Trade Area of the Americas (FTAA) in Belo Horizonte, Brazil. Between June and August, a new International Meeting for Humanity and Against Neoliberalism was held in Barcelona, proposing the organization of Peoples' Global Action, which launched eight months later. In October, in the midst of the Asian financial crisis, Jubilee 2000, made up of Christian and social organizations, formed and initiated a campaign to cancel poor countries' external debt.

In February 1998, at the same time that the OECD was making its MAI proposal official, a campaign against the accord was launched. In April, a People's Summit of the Americas, as a CSA activity, was held parallel to the Second Presidential Summit of the Americas. During this month, the first protests against the OECD, which was leading the approval of the MAI, also took place in Paris. Following this, during the second annual meeting of the G-7 in Birmingham, England, we witnessed a demonstration of seventy thousand people, organized by Jubilee 2000, for the cancellation of poor countries' debts. Protests were repeated at the Second Ministerial Meeting of the WTO, held in Geneva. On July 3, a citizens' movement, ATTAC, was formed in France. ATTAC advocated a campaign to promote taxation of international financial transactions (the Tobin tax). After this, in the second half of the year, protests against the MAI were held in different countries, until the OECD decided in October to suspend negotiations of the accord.

The year 1999 began with the organization of the international meeting "Another Davos" in Zurich, Switzerland, held simultaneously with the meeting of the World Economic Forum, which brought together businesspeople and governments. ATTAC, the World Alternatives Forum, Coordination against the MAI, and Structural Adjustment Participatory Review International Network, which promoted the alternative

---

The Multilateral Agreement on Investment

Negotiations to create the Multilateral Agreement on Investment (MAI) began in 1995. They were held secretly by the world's richest nations, led by G-7 members, without the knowledge of citizens or their elected officials. There was a clear desire to ensure that the public remained ignorant. By early 1997, almost 90 percent of the proposal was already in what could have been its final form. The MAI would have created international investment legislation, based on the interests of central countries and their transnational corporations, removing from each country the possibility of legislating investment-related issues. The agreement was planned as a type of world constitution for capital, giving practically all of the rights, without any obligations, to investors. In this sense, the OECD was chosen to be the world headquarters, and not the WTO, because it was a discreet organization that would not enable the participation of developing countries or other spectators.

event, began working at this meeting, with the idea of "another globalization." These same groups returned to meet, together with others, in June, at the international meeting "Another World Is Possible," held in Paris. On June 18, Reclaim the Streets organized a demonstration of ten thousand young people in London against the domination of finance capital—which surprised the police and managed to paralyze "The City," the English financial center, for the first time since 1850. On October 12, the first Latin American "Cry of the Excluded," whose slogan was "For Work, Justice and Life," took place, expressing a change in the political-ideological climate

---

The world media had closely followed the earlier WTO negotiations and could have publicized objections to the MAI negotiations. The first alerts about the agreement were released in Ottawa, Washington, New York, San Francisco, and Geneva by nongovernmental organizations that were active in the spheres of economic and social development, defense of human rights, and the environment. From there, a network of associations began to dissect the agreement text and engage in an information and mobilization campaign. The proposal for the MAI was released to the public at the beginning of 1998. The organization Public Citizen, in an article by attorney Lori Wallach, denounced the agreement. Following this, the French journal *Le Monde Diplomatique* gave ample coverage to these denunciations. The reaction to the extraordinary proposals in the agreement made possible the creation of a social protest movement, which forced France to withdraw from the project, impeding the continuity of the negotiation process. Many of its clauses, however, continue to be negotiated in the confines of the WTO and the FTAA.

and a return to social mobilizations in the region. On November 18–20, the International Meeting for Abolition of the Third World Debt and the South-South Summit on the debt was held in Johannesburg, South Africa.

These are just some of the activities with the largest repercussions, giving rise to international campaigns, marches, and protests. What happened in Seattle would not be an isolated episode, but rather a catalyst for profound and ongoing developments.

CHAPTER TWO

From Seattle to Genoa: The Protest Cycle

The global movement, a "movement" into which all other movements converge, is the result of new political practices, constituted through a growing cycle of international protests against those institutions that attempt to administer neoliberal globalization. Vast coalitions, networks, and movements worldwide horizontally organized the global movement. Simultaneously, they sought to construct an affirmative identity—a sense of what they were *for*—coming together in many meetings and countersummits, until the World Social Forum brought them together.

However, none of this would have been possible without the initial catalyzing event, the Seattle protests against the World Trade Organization (WTO).

SEATTLE AS A FOUNDING EVENT

On November 30, 1999, fifty thousand demonstrators took over the streets in Seattle, protesting against the third ministerial meeting of the WTO, which was supposed to consolidate earlier discussions held at the Singapore (December 1996) and Geneva (May 1998) meetings. The conference would have inaugurated the so-called Millennium Round, a new negotiation cycle for trade liberalization focused on agriculture and services (education, health, environmental, and cultural activities). But the demonstrators blocked the Seattle streets and forced the cancellation of important parts of the meeting, making visible to the world not only the existence of an opposition to neoliberal globalization but the possibility of contesting and reversing it. The protests produced a massive media event and a major political event, which catalyzed the different movements and organizations, making it possible from that moment on for movements to view themselves as part of the same process.

For this action, 1,449 organizations in 89 countries had signed an appeal, coordinated by the English division of the environmental group Friends of the Earth. The appeal called for a moratorium on negotiations and demanded that the WTO be given no new powers without a prior evaluation of the application of free-trade policies—including intellectual property agreements, which regulate patents and are viewed as increasingly decisive—implemented since the signing of agreements in Marrakech that founded the WTO in 1995. The activists from these hundreds of organizations prepared and staged the Battle of Seattle.

The protests were planned diligently and over a long period of time. As Susan George writes:

> The civic movement's success in Seattle is a mystery only to those who had no part in it. Throughout 1999, thanks primarily to the Internet, tens of thousands of people opposed to

the World Trade Organisation (WTO) united in a great national and international effort of organisation. Anyone could have a front seat, anyone could take part in the advance on Seattle. All you needed was a computer and a rough knowledge of English.

Within the North American context, the key factor favoring the mobilization's success was what was called the Sweeney-Greenie alliance, representing the new AFL-CIO leadership under the presidency of John Sweeney and the ecologists (greens), who in 2000 launched Ralph Nader as a Green Party presidential candidate. In that election, Nader received nearly three million votes, a large number for a candidate who was not part of the U.S. bipartisan system. An additional strategic element was the growing engagement of university students in the United States in what they called the Global Justice Movement, whose most visible activist focus was the "No Sweats" campaign, combating sweatshops.

An Internet list, Stop the WTO Round, became an important instrument for international and national organization of the broad and fluid coalition that organized the demonstration, unprecedented in its diversity. Activists from Public Citizen, Ralph Nader's and Lori Wallach's organization, spent months laying the groundwork for the demonstrators. The Direct Action Network (and the Ruckus Society) trained thousands of activists in the nonviolent direct-action techniques used in the protests (the conference center's perimeter was divided into thirteen zones, and for each one, a group, including people who, if necessary, were willing to be arrested, was charged with blocking passage). Cultural groups produced huge marionettes and puppets, staged dances, street theater, and hip-hop and rap concerts, which gave the protests a festive air, according to the new standard of radical youth mobilization. From November 26 to November 29, in San Francisco, the International Forum on Globalization (IFG) promoted a large international seminar on the theme, with 2,500 participants helping to heat up the debate.

All social sectors could be receptive to a debate on the WTO because of the breadth of its decisions, which affect every aspect of social life. The case of the marine turtles is an example. The North American environmental movement was very conscious of the huge threat that the WTO represented

---

The World Trade Organization

The World Trade Organization was established on January 1, 1995, at the end of the Uruguay Round of the GATT (General Agreement on Tariffs and Trade), which lasted from 1986 to 1994. This agreement functioned through negotiation rounds, in which the countries negotiated bilaterally or in blocs that established accords. In the first rounds after the Second World War, the principal negotiations focused on customs tariffs reductions and only later began to include issues such as anti-dumping and nontariff barriers. The negotiations were focused on trade liberalization, but unlike the WTO, the GATT was an instance of negotiations between nations that may or may not have reached agreement.

With the institution of the WTO, according to the Marrakech agreement signed by 120 countries on April 14, 1994, a truly international organization was created that acts as an administrator of trade deals, a negotiation forum, and a space for set-to environmental laws because of a decision by the organization to banish, as an unjust trade barrier, a clause in North American legislation covering endangered species. The clause demanded that shrimp fishing be conducted using devices to avoid the accidental capture of turtles in nets. This became one of the emblems of the Seattle protests. Because the ministerial meeting started on Earth Day, the Earth Island Institute prepared five hundred marine turtle costumes for the demonstrators, whose visual impact was felt all week long in the city. One of the principal protest chroniclers, Jeffrey St. Clair, during the environmental protests that inau- >

---

tling trade disputes and reviewing national trade policies. The WTO is an organization with powers to sanction countries that do not conform to its norms, and it also acts as an arbiter of trade guidelines, with a view to reducing tariffs and opening markets, in cooperation with the IMF and World Bank. With the intensification of the globalization process, WTO action has grown over the past decade. The expansion of commercial trade on the international level transformed the WTO into one of the most influential supranational organizations of our times. However, differences in power among member states persists.

On the issue of agriculture, developing countries called for an end to subsidies provided by the United States and European Union to their agricultural sectors, which have the effect of undermining the competitiveness of poor countries' products in European and North American markets. However, the poor countries were required to remove export subsidies on agricultural products, reducing their competitiveness even more. The system policing world trade is subordinated to the power differ- >

gurated the demonstrations, heard a labor union member say one of the phrases that best symbolized Seattle's novelty: "Teamsters and Turtles Together at Last!"

The new movement's broad reach, and its open and internationalist character, can be clearly seen in the following list of speakers at street demonstrations and teach-ins around the city: "Martin Khor and Vandana Shiva of the Third World Network in Asia, Walden Bello of Focus on the Global South, Maude Barlow of the Council of Canadians, Tony Clarke of Polaris Institute, Jerry Mander of the International Forum on Globalization, Susan George of the Transnational Institute, David Korten of the People-Centered Development Forum, John Cavanagh of the Institute for Policy Studies, Lori Wallach of Public Citizen, Mark Ritchie of the Institute for Agriculture and Trade Policy, Anuradha Mittal of the Institute for Food and Development Policy, Helena Norberg-Hodge of the International Society for Ecology and Culture, Owens Wiwa

---

ences between countries: the WTO removes the central management of trade policies from the hands of national governments of developing countries, putting the policies into an arena dominated by the rich countries' interests. These disputes led to the failure of the Third Ministerial Conference of the WTO, held at the end of 1999 in Seattle. Its objective was to start the Millennium Round, in which total trade liberalization would have been discussed. At the fourth conference in Doha, Qatar, in November 2001, the new round was finally imposed and should be evaluated in the fifth conference in Cancun, Mexico in September 2003.

of the Movement for the Survival of the Ogoni People, Chakravarthi Raghavan of the Third World Network in Geneva, Debra Harry of the Indigenous Peoples Coalition Against Biopiracy, José Bové of the Confederation Paysanne ..., Tetteh Hormoku of the Third World Network in Africa."[*]

As such, all of the conditions for the Battle of Seattle, which the media presented to the world as an inaugural act of the movement they would call "antiglobalization," were in place.

In their book *Resistencias mundiales* (Worldwide Resistances), José Seoane and Emilio Taddei write:

> On November 30, the Battle of Seattle blocked the streets. Thousands of students marched to the city center. Thousands of ecologists, feminists, farmers and growers, human rights activists added their protests to WTO policies. The streets were blocked by the "Seattle turtles"; by students staging sit-ins in front of the official delegations' hotels, and above all, around the Convention Center, where the opening ceremony of the Millennium Round was planned. The police savagely repressed them, using rubber bullets and pepper gas, and the famous images of the demonstrators dressed as green turtles spread around the world. Memorial Stadium was the stage for the giant Labor Rally, in which 30,000 union members participated. At the closing of the action, 50,000 marched through the streets of Seattle, forcing the failure of the WTO meeting opening and blocking meetings in hotels. All night long, a real battle blew up in the streets, where thousands of activists were arrested. The street protests and repression lasted until December 3, a moment at which the differences at the WTO's heart erupted, and numerous Third World representatives raised their voices against the negotiations of industrialized countries and the

---

[*] From Paul G. Hawken, "A Report from the WTO/Seattle Conference," January 6, 2000, available online at http://www.global-vision.org/misc/hawken1.html.

"millennium farce." The meeting's failure exacerbated the trade controversies between the United States and European Union. On Thursday, December 4, the local newspaper, the *Seattle Times,* ran a headline "Talks Collapse; Meeting Ends—Groups Will Leave Here Without An Agreement." The Millennium Rounds had sunk.[*]

Seoane and Taddei remember that the Battle of Seattle

was a great mark of social protest in the United States. It was the most important demonstration in North American society since the years of protest against the Vietnam War. But, in addition to this, Seattle crystallized the convergence, even with inclinations and differences, of the North American labor movement with movements of environmentalists, peasants, consumer defenders, feminists, and protestors against Third World debt. The convergence of the North American labor movement with foreign unions and diverse social movements materialized on the streets. Many North American labor leaders marched alongside delegates from the French CGT and SUD, the Brazilian CUT, Korean KCTU, the South African COSATU, farmer representatives, women, students, and ecologists. This was unprecedented in the postwar North American labor movement, known for the furious anticommunism of the AFL-CIO and its profound suspicion of any radical movement.

In this sense, the days of protest against the WTO demonstrated to the world the emergence of a radical and democratic movement in the United States, which upon new foundations and issues (ecology, denouncing of social dumping practices in the Third World by North American transnationals, etc.) have recalled the experience of movements in the 1960s and 1970s.

On a worldwide scale, Seattle was a "baptism by fire" and a moment of consolidation of this vast, diverse and new

---

[*] From José Seoane and Emilio Taddei, "De Seattle a Porto Alegre: Pasado, presente y futuro del movimiento anti-mundialización neoliberal," in Seoane, J. and Taddei, E., eds. *Resistencias Mundiales* (Buenos Aires: CLASCO, 2001), 113.

global movement against injustice. Seattle was unthinkable without the previous battles, and its unexpected eruption into the media contrasted with the ample and methodical activist work that was conducted for months in order to "to astonish the world and advance the arrival of the millennium."

Seattle represented a qualitative leap in the trajectory of resistance to neoliberal globalization, a moment in which a group of activists lost the illusion that it was possible to work in harmony with the multilateral institutions. The collaborative character of their initiatives ended. In this radicalization, the most disparate initiatives were able to converge in a movement against ongoing globalization. It is not a coincidence that the focus of this rupture had been the key meeting of the WTO, the institution more unwilling than any to change its rhetoric to acknowledge its critics and whose formation in 1995 symbolized both the liberation of capital from national control and the tyranny of global capitalism made insane by greed.

The result surpassed the expectations of even the most optimistic organizers. The five-day protests resulted in the suspension of the conference's opening ceremony; impeded President Bill Clinton's speech to WTO delegates on the night of the gala; created a huge upset in the media, which had to recognize the popular support for the demonstrations against the organization; forced the WTO to cancel its closing ceremony, without an agenda for continuity; and catalyzed the conflicts and divergences between the countries whose delegates participated in the meeting. The media impact of the protests was gigantic. Seattle became a symbol of a U-turn in the political situation and a foundational event that established the global movement as a permanent actor on the scene.

THE PROTESTS, FROM WASHINGTON TO GENOA

Seattle kicked off an increasingly vigorous protest cycle that consolidated the global movement. At each new meeting of the IMF, the World Bank, the G-7 or the G-8, the OECD, and the World Economic Forum, as well as at the European Union summits and the negotiations for the FTAA, the governments and globalized capitalist elite came under siege in their fortresses and palaces by the movements seeking justice and rights. The constantly renewed protests against market tyranny had a powerful political and symbolic impact, undermining the legitimacy of the institutions responsible for neoliberal globalization, impelling the convergence of battles into one great, practical, plural, multifaceted movement with an increasing ability to unite. Each new mobilization tended to strengthen the movement, broadening its social bases and creating the conditions for new, even stronger protests.

Simultaneously, newly formed or already existing movements gained an international dimension and staged counter-summits, conferences, or alternative assemblies in addition to their network and organizational conferences. Discussions multiplied on specific issues (water, trade, AIDS, offshore tax havens, food security, control of financial capital). The movement also began to promote even larger meetings, of which the World Social Forum became central and the reference point for the entire process.

Walden Bello said that 2000 was the year of global protest against "globalization" of capital, but the marches established in the Seattle mobilizations continued to crescendo until the gigantic protests around the G-8 meeting in Genoa, Italy, in July 2001. This expanding cycle was interrupted only by the terrorist attacks on September 11, 2001. At that time, protests were being organized against the joint meeting in Washington, D.C., of the IMF and World Bank, scheduled for the end of September, and against the Fourth WTO Ministerial Conference at the beginning of November in Doha, Qatar—relocated there to make demonstrations more difficult. The attacks on the World Trade Center and Pentagon brought with them an important change in the world political situation, which altered as much the focus as the conditions of protests, which began to incorporate a struggle against militarization and war.

During this interim period, dozens of significant demonstrations carried the Seattle protests forward. Some were already organized before Seattle took place, such the meeting in opposition to the World Social Forum in Davos ("The Other Davos") in January, and on the occasion of the Tenth Summit of the United Nations Conference on Trade and Development in Bangkok, Thailand. On March 8, the World March of Women 2000 began, culminating on October 17 with the delivery to UN headquarters of a petition that contained five million signatures supporting demands to combat poverty and sexist violence. The march promoted important demonstrations in Brussels (50,000 women), in Ottawa (more than 50,000), in Brasilia (20,000 rural workers), and at the final assembly in New York (10,000 women).

The global movement's second great assembly was the April 16 protest in Washington, D.C., at the spring meeting of the IMF and World Bank. On this occasion, more than thirty thousand protesters were present, representing a movement coalition that attempted to re-create the Seattle process. Again AFL-CIO union members were featured, mainly steelworkers and those from the communications sector, as well as youth, organized into affinity groups and coordinated in "spokescouncils," or open assemblies of activists. Also playing an important role were activists from Jobs with Justice, an organization created to promote community solidarity with workers' struggles, and the diverse NGOs involved in the fight against corporate globalization.

In subsequent months, new protests were staged: in Chiang Mai, Thailand, in May, at the annual meeting of the Asian Development Bank; in Geneva, Switzerland, June 22–25, at the Alternative Summit to the Second Summit on Social Development organized by the United Nations (when the proposal first arose to convene the World Social Forum in Porto Alegre as a countersummit to the World Economic Forum in Davos); in Millau, France, on June 20 and July 1, when thirty thousand people protested the lawsuit against José Bové and other activists from the Peasants Confederation for dismantling a McDonald's; in Okinawa, Japan, June 21–23, during the meeting of the G-7, demanding the abolition of Third World debt and the removal of North American military bases from the country.

The height of the 2000 protests was the month of September. The protests started in New York, on September 8, during the UN Millennium Meeting. On September 11, in Melbourne, Australia, a huge demonstration was called against a regional meeting of the World Economic Forum. A cordon of twenty thousand protesters blocked some of the delegations from entering the meeting location. And, on September 26 in Prague, the Czech Republic, on the occasion of the annual IMF and World Bank meeting, which attracted twenty thousand bankers and international bureaucrats, twenty thousand demonstrators participated in protests that sparked speculation on one day that the meeting would be canceled. Youth delegations from almost every country in Europe were there, including one thousand Spanish and five hundred German and Swiss protesters, but there was little union presence. Anarchists and activists from the most important leftist groups, green parties, and communists made a strong appearance. For the first time in Europe, the tactics developed for Seattle were used: strong organizing via the Internet, the establishment of a convergence center, the organization of demonstrators into affinity groups, attempts to block the meeting, and systematic confrontation with the police. The organizations that attended, such as the Euromarches against Unemployment, Jubilee 2000, ATTAC, 50 Years Is Enough!, and Focus on the Global South, staged a countersummit, which adopted the following declaration:

> So long as that model continues to be imposed by the rich and the powerful, organizations like ours shall continue to protest and to do everything in our power to expose the plain failures of the system. Wherever those who have taken upon themselves the power to make decisions for the global economy will gather, we will be there to witness, to expose, and to protest.

On September 26, protests also occurred in forty other countries.

On December 5–6, the European Union Summit, held at the Acropolis in Nice, France, was the site of massive demonstrations against the neoliberal policy of unifying the continent. Here, for the first time, there was a strong presence of unions from all over Europe, marching alongside social movements, youth organizations, and leftist parties. It is significant that in The Hague, The Netherlands, almost simultaneously, the Convention on Climate Change failed in its attempts to save the Kyoto Protocol and counter the trends toward global warming by gas emissions, making ever greater concessions to the United States.

The first World Social Forum, held January 25–30, 2001, in Porto Alegre, Brazil, galvanized the different movements and networks that gathered seeking to debate the neoliberal world and alternatives to it as well as to coordinate their actions and protests. Here the Social Movements International Secretariat met and formulated its document titled "Porto Alegre Call for Mobilization," which approved a protest agenda. The conclusion of its text states:

> We commit ourselves to support all the struggles of our common agenda to mobilise opposition to neoliberalism. Among our priorities for the coming months, we will mobilize globally against the:
>
> - World Economic Forum, Cancun, Mexico, 26 and 27 February
> - Free Trade Area of the Americas, Buenos Aires, Argentina, 6–7 April, and Quebec City, Canada, 17–22 April
> - Asian Development Bank, Honolulu, May
> - G8 Summit, Genoa, Italy, 15–22 July
> - IMF and World Bank Annual Meeting, Washington DC, USA, 28 September–4 October
> - World Trade Organisation, 5–9 November (Qatar?)

The chronology of central protests for the year was not followed exactly, but Porto Alegre facilitated the movement's ability to project itself, its sense of identity, and its common purpose. On March 15, in Naples, Italy, more than forty thousand people protested at the Third Global Forum Fostering Democracy and Development through E-Government, illustrating the Italians' sensitivity to the fight against neoliberal globalization. On April 5–6, twelve thousand demonstrators came together in Buenos Aires, Argentina, against the FTAA meeting. At the end of the month, many staged a large protest in Quebec, Canada, against the Summit of the Americas, a meeting of national presidents from the countries of the Americas. Thousands of global justice activists staged a People's Summit of the Americas. When they marched on the ministerial meeting, they were confronted—for the first time at a global summit—with a large barrier encircling the meeting location. Between June 22 and June 25, the Barcelona Social Forum was held. It would have been staged simultaneously with the canceled World Bank meeting, and it witnessed an important demonstration. At nearly the same time, more than twenty thousand activists protested against the meeting of European Union heads of state and a visit by U.S. president George Bush at the summit in Göteborg, Sweden.

When the G-8 met in Genoa, Italy, at the beginning of July, the largest protest to date, involving around 300,000 demonstrators, took place. On the other side, the right-wing government of Silvio Berlusconi was firmly resolved to face the movement, preparing to strongly repress the demonstrators, in line with the policy of central governments criminalizing demonstrations. It presented the protests as acts of vandalism by those in the minority. The organizers of the Genoa Social Forum, held just before the demonstrations and inspired by the

World Social Forum (the leaders having met in Porto Alegre), were able to build a broad coalition of every type of movement, employing a vast European-scale mobilization. It strongly challenged police brutality and contrasted with the isolation of the government representatives, none of whom could add anything concrete to the G-8 meeting, the first in which Bush participated, already reflecting the U.S. government's unilateralist turn. The repression of the protests ended in the murder of a young demonstrator, Carlo Giuliani, by Italian police. The movement faced and won a battle for public opinion for which the neoliberal governments had prepared for months.

The One Idea System
By Ignacio Ramonet

Bogged down. In today's democracies, an increasing number of free citizens feel bogged down, glued down by a kind of sticky dogma that is in the process of surreptitiously engulfing any contrary way of thinking by inhibiting it, by disturbing it, by paralysing it and in the end, by squeezing it shut. This dogma is the One Idea System, the only idea allowed by an invisible but nevertheless omnipresent opinion police.

Since the fall of the Berlin Wall, the collapse of the communist regimes, and the socialist movement's generalised loss of self-confidence, the arrogance, impudence and haughtiness of this new Gospel have reached such heights that one can safely characterise this ideological frenzy by the name of modern dogmatism.

What is the One Idea system? It is the translation into allegedly universal ideological premises of the interests of an as-

We are, therefore, far from a situation in which what Ignacio Ramonet calls "the one idea" promoted aggressively by neoliberalism appears to drown out all criticism and make people accept the commercialization of life, culture, and the world. Since Seattle, the worldwide movement against corporate globalization energizes young people, inspires hopes, reestablishes utopias, and reconstructs a sense of the possibility of history made by real human beings, by their choices and struggles. Against the barrage of market worship, which numbs human consciousness into believing that capitalism is the natural state of society, a new movement and a new militant generation has >

---

semblage of economic forces (actors?), especially those (represented by) international capital. As a matter of fact, the One Idea System had already been defined and announced at Bretton Woods in 1944. It mostly originates from the big monetary and economic institutions such as the World Bank, the International Monetary Fund, the OECD, the GATT, the European Commission, the Bank of France, etc. By providing research money and other funds these institutions (are able to) sign up numerous research centres, universities, and foundations across the globe. These, in turn, refine and disseminate the Gospel.

This anonymous discourse is then picked up and reproduced by the main providers of economic information, most prominently by the bankers', stockbrokers' and investors' favorite papers: *The Wall Street Journal*, *The Financial Times*, *The Economist*, *The Far Eastern Review*, *Les Echos*, Reuters, etc. For the most part, big industrial or financial groups own these organs. And almost everywhere, university economics departments, journalists, >

presented a field of ideas and a space for political action in which another world could be possible, if we fight for it.

The correlation of social forces remains hostile to popular forces overall: capitalism holds the initiatives and a significant part of the bourgeoisie has aligned with ultraconservative leaders, such as Bush and Berlusconi. However, time does not stand still, and a *historical turning point* was realized on the streets of Seattle. In the movement's development, the potential was raised for a much greater mobilization of forces, for the precipitation of an open crisis of neoliberal globalization, and for the construction of global alternatives.

---

essayists and politicians make these new Ten Commandments their own, and recite them ad nauseam through the mass media. All in the knowledge that in our age of thoroughly media-dominated societies, repetition means proof.

The leading premise of the One Idea System is all the more powerful since (avowedly absent-minded) Marxists would not contradict it. It states that the economic sphere takes precedence over the political one. It is on the basis of this very premise that, to take but one example, a major political instrument such as the (Reserve) Bank of France was made independent (of the government) in 1994, and this without noticeable opposition. The Bank has been, as they say, "removed from the vagaries of politics". "The Bank of France is independent, non-political, and cuts across the parties" states its CEO, Jean Claude Trichet, only to add: "We do however ask (the government) to reduce the budget deficit (and) we do pursue a stable currency strategy". As if these objectives were anything but political objectives!... It is in the name of (this same) "realism" and

In a process a radical new political-programmatic agenda emerged, with imprecise contours but some points of convergence and clear demands, expressing diffuse anticapitalist sentiments and establishing a foundation for debating concrete alternatives. This agenda—which includes annulling poor countries' debts, questioning intellectual property rights, defending cultural diversity, controlling the flow of transnational capital, decommercialization of spheres of social life, and establishing spaces for rights and benefits—is the result of neoliberal globalization's own issues. It is also a product of new forces that participated in the movement, >

"pragmatism" that Mr Alain Minc comes to the following statement: "Capitalism will not collapse, because capitalism is the natural state of society. Democracy is not the natural state of society. The market is at the helm". And of course we're talking here of an economy that has been "freed" from the embarrassment of the social sphere [i.e. concern for jobs, education, health care, etc.], that horrible and pathetic straightjacket which stands accused of being the root cause of our recessions and economic crises.

Other key features of the One Idea System are well known: The market, that deity whose "invisible hand corrects the disparities and dysfunctions of capitalism", and then most of all, the financial markets, whose "signals guide and determine the general trends of the economy"; competition and competitivity, that "stimulate and dynamise enterprises, by keeping them in a process of permanent and beneficial modernisation"; borderless free trade, "a source of an unending increase of commercial exchanges, and thus of the development of society"; >

whether linked to the social movements born in the 1960s (environmentalists, antiracists, feminists) or a new political generation that emerged in the 1990s in opposition to globalized neoliberal capitalism.

In 2001, before the September 11 attacks, it was clear that the global movement represented, in some countries, a significant recomposition of the Left. In the United States, this was already being expressed in youth activism, in the growth of activist networks, and in the large coalition that supported Ralph Nader's 2000 presidential campaign. In Italy, the political radicalization was expressed in mass activism, but it also was reflected in support for the Communist Refoundation Party. In France and England, the formation of new organizations, such as ATTAC, combined with a crisis in the Left's political representation and a larger audience for radical left

---

globalization, both of industrial production and of financial flows; international division of labour, which "keep the unions' demands in check and lowers the costs of labour"; strong currency, "an (important) stabilising factor"; deregulation; privatisation; liberalisation, etc. "Less and less State", a permanent arbitration in favour of incomes deriving from capital above those deriving from work. And an absolute disregard for all ecological consequences.

The constant reiteration of this new catechism in all the media by almost all politicians, whether they belong to the left or to the right, endows it with such an intimidating power that it stifles any attempt to think freely about it, and renders next to impossible any opposition against this new obscurantism.

One would almost come to think that the 17.4 million jobless

organizations. Everywhere the movement federated and regrouped existing organizations into broad networks.

Europeans, the collapse of the inner cities, the widespread sentiment of insecurity and marginalization, the generalised corruption, the riots in the highrise ghettos of the urban peripheries, the environmental carnage, the return of religious, political and racist extremism, and the rising tide of the excluded are mere phantasms, nay, are criminal hallucinations, which culpably disrupt the envisioning of that most marvellous of all possible worlds which is being built for us and our anaesthetised consciences by the One Idea System.

Originally published in Le Monde Diplomatique, *January 1995. Translated by Patrice Riemens, University of Amsterdam. Reprinted with permission.*

CHAPTER THREE

The World Social Forum: A Political Invention

At the beginning of 2000, while the shock waves of Seattle still echoed throughout the world, a group of Brazilians proposed a plan to help the movement opposed to corporate globalization reach a new stage by organizing the World Social Forum. The resistance movements were undertaking various organizing initiatives, but these had as a focus the World Economic Forum in Davos and its key role in the formulation and practice of world domination by capital.

Francisco Whitaker elaborated on the proposal in an article written at the end of 2000:

> Well, in the light of all this that was going on, a few Brazilians decided that it would be possible to launch a new stage of resistance to the school of thought which today prevails all over the world. Over and beyond the demonstrations and mass protests, though, it seemed possible to move on and to offer specific proposals, to seek concrete responses to the challenges of building "another world," one where the economy would serve people, and not the other way round. Economists and other academics opposed to neoliberalism were

already holding what they called Anti-Davos meetings in Europe. Now though, the intention was to go further than that. The idea was, with the participation of all the organizations that were already networking in the mass protests, to arrange another kind of meeting on a world scale—the World Social Forum—directed to social concerns. To give a symbolic dimension to the start of this new period, the meeting would take place on the same dates as the powerful of the world were to meet in Davos.

Exactly who had this great idea? Our friend Oded Grajew—I don't know if he discussed it with anyone else beforehand—but he put it to me when we met in France in February this year. Together, we decided to take it to Bernard Cassen, director of *Le Monde Diplomatique,* who is also president of ATTAC in France, to see how well the idea would be received outside of Brazil.

Cassen was enthusiastic and made the proposal to hold the Forum in Brazil. He felt it had to be in the "Third World"—because that would also have a symbolic effect—and Brazil was among the countries in a better position to host a Forum like this. His too was the idea of hosting it in Porto Alegre, capital of a state that is steadily becoming known all over the world for its democratic experiences and efforts against neoliberalism. Cassen then threw out a counter-challenge: if we were able to organize the Forum, we would have the support not only of his newspaper, but also of the organizations around the world that are positioning themselves against domination by capital.

Once back in Brazil, we started to find out what organizations were willing to accept this challenge and take on this huge task. On February 28, there was a meeting in São Paulo of delegates from 8 organizations that today have signed a "Cooperation Agreement" to hold the World Social Forum, the first edition of which will be held in Porto Alegre from January 25 to 30, 2001:

> Brazilian Association of Non-Governmental Organizations (ABONG); Association for the Taxation of Financial Transactions for the Aid of Citizens (ATTAC);

Brazilian Justice & Peace Commission (CBJP); Brazilian Business Association for Citizenship (CIVES); Central Trade Union Federation (CUT); Brazilian Institute for Social and Economic Studies (IBASE); Center for Global Justice (CJG); Landless Rural Workers Movement (MST).

In March these organizations sent a delegation to Porto Alegre to consult Rio Grande do Sul Governor Olívio Dutra and Porto Alegre Mayor Raul Pont on the state and municipal governments' willingness to host the Forum, on the understanding that the event would be promoted not by these governments, but by the civil society organizations that embraced the proposal. Once the governor and mayor had given their consent, work was begun as quickly as possible to organize and actually realize this new world meeting. This included inviting other civil society organizations to set up a Brazilian Committee in Support of the Forum.

At Cassen's suggestion, a delegation from the organizations traveled in late June to Geneva where a large part of the organizations linking up around the world in demonstrations against neoliberalism would be meeting in an alternative "summit" parallel to the UN's "Copenhagen + 5" Summit. Room was made for us to present our proposal, which was very well received. Miguel Rossetto, Deputy Governor of Rio Grande do Sul state, also traveled to Geneva to confirm that the state would host the Forum. On that very occasion, an International Committee was set up in support of the Forum.[*]

Before the protests on June 25 against the Social Development Summit, a conference was held June 22–24 in Geneva with five hundred representatives of the movements opposed to neoliberal globalization. This conference had been called February 12 at a meeting in Bangkok, Thailand, where protests were held

---

[*] "World Social Forum: Origin and Aims," translated from the Portuguese by Peter Lenny.

against the United Nations Conference on Trade and Development, and was being prepared by a Swiss support committee and ATTAC France.

At the conference, the Brazilian Organizing Committee presented the text of the proposal:

> The World Social Forum will be a new international space for reflection and for organization of all those who counter neoliberal policies and are constructing alternatives to prioritize human development and overcome market domination in every country and in international relations.

Directed at NGOs, social movements, unions, and religious associations, the World Social Forum seeks "the identification of paths and mobilizing proposals for demonstrations and concrete actions of civil society." In the proposal, the forum appears as a consequence of the ongoing demonstrations, the struggles against the MAI and the Seattle protests, which "definitively made evident the emergence of a civic movement reaching beyond national borders." Thousands of movements and entities involved in isolated battles

> became conscious that, together, they constituted a planetary archipelago of resistance to neoliberal globalization. They began to get to know each other, regularly exchanging information, uniting in common actions and convergences, starting to concretize a vocation, which could become a planetary counter-power of citizens.

In the organizing section of the document, the proposal's format already began to be designed:

> The WSF will include three types of activities: I) a series of daily plenary sessions, with speeches and expositions by invited personalities; II) the greatest number possible of meetings for presenting ongoing initiatives and to exchange

experiences; III) organizing and articulation meetings among social organizations that develop the same types of struggles. The plenary sessions will be scheduled by WSF organizers, according to themes to be defined; the encounters and meetings will be scheduled based upon the interests and requests of the WSF participants.

It was also established that WSF participants would be "representatives of NGOs, unions, social movements, citizens' groups, speakers and those who held elected mandates," registered by their organizations, and leaving aside political parties. It was defined with a "spatial" character and not as a forum organization:

The World Social Forum is not a moment for deliberation about the theses and proposals presented there. The participants, overall, will have clear freedom to make decisions, disseminate proposals and take positions resulting from their specific organizing meetings.

The document proposed at the meeting in Geneva also foresaw the constitution of an International WSF Committee, which was formed one year later. The proposal received broad support in Geneva from movements already involved in the dynamic of international coordination of struggles, integrating entities such as French ATTAC and the journal *Le Monde Diplomatique*, the World Forum for Alternatives, Focus on the Global South, and Via Campesina. This initial sponsorship was also strengthened by the support of Latin American groups and movements, for example, the Continental Social Alliance, the Latin American Council of Social Sciences (CLACSO), and the Latin America Information Agency (ALAI).

Organizing moved forward with many uncertainties about the event's size and shape. However, the state and municipal governments' support reinforced the event's organization and made available an excellent infrastructure in the buildings of the Pontifical Catholic University (PUC) of Rio Grande do Sul in Porto Alegre. As the forum drew near, a large support network composed of activists formed throughout the state, enabling the Brazilian Organizing Committee, with the support of local officials, to overcome all difficulties. The forum became an initiative backed by the state's civil society, by organizations and movements representing the large social base of Rio Grande do Sul's Left, and brought about the formation of the large State Organizing Committee.

The proposal for the WSF appeared at the right time with the right format for a movement in clear ascendancy: an open event in a Third World city, identified with the Brazilian Workers' Party (PT), and considered by many to have had the most advanced experience in constructing alternatives to neoliberalism. What was more, the city and state provided strong political and organizational backup.

THE FIRST WORLD SOCIAL FORUM

Using the slogan "Another World Is Possible," 4,000 delegates, 16,000 registered participants from 117 countries, 1,870 journalists (with 386 foreigners), as well as an unknown number of walk-in participants attended activities January 25–30, 2001, of the first World Social Forum on the PUC campus in Porto Alegre. They participated in 16 plenary sessions, 400 workshops, and 20 testimonials in the strict sense of the WSF, and in a large number of autonomous activities, held simultaneously in the city, such as the World Parliamentary Forum, the Forum of Local Authorities for Social Inclusion, the Intercontinental Youth Camp (with 2,400 participants), the Indigenous Peoples Camp (with 700 participants), and many parallel meetings, marches, demonstrations, concerts, cultural activities, and parties.

This surprising attendance, much larger than organizers expected, was one of the indicators of the event's success. The outcome of the assembled activities, which signified the forum's multifaceted and pluralistic character, embodying the spirit of the worldwide movement's battle against neoliberalism, was an important morale boost. It represented a rupture in the "one idea" system and a chance to connect to an enormous diversity of social and political actors and debates. It helped to promote struggles and to build a greater political identity among those who sought an alternative to neoliberalism. For French ATTAC members, militants from the landless movement MST, union members from South Korea, anarcho-punks from Rio Grande do Sul, Quebec nationalists, and all those fighting the FTAA in Latin America, the forum demonstrated that they were not alone in their concerns and struggles.

The forum galvanized the spirit of the protests that had been shadowing meetings of multinational organizations and helped to reverse the international political and ideological climate. Though a large majority of the participants were Brazilian, the main groups involved in the protests in worldwide sent representatives to Porto Alegre. Those participants gave an international dimension to the World Social Forum and, in practice, acted as its nerve center.

An intense agenda of discussions and political meetings characterized the forum. Regional meetings by continent (except for Latin America) and sector meetings were held to organize the new fights against capitalist globalization. Via Campesina coordinated more than eighty peasant organizations from around the world and held a huge plenary session. Unions also met during the forum. The women's movement had great visibility at the event. The NGOs that participated in the forum, particularly the Brazilian NGOs, were rejuvenated by the discussions, as Jorge Durão wrote:

> [F]or the NGOs, Porto Alegre and its aftermath represented an extraordinary opportunity for intellectual exposure.... For good or bad, the NGOs have been frequently tangled up in ideological discussions about development ... and they have much to gain through dialogue with an wide variety of interlocutors, above all with those who come from the intellectual world, which does not renounce the criticism of capitalism nor allow itself to be intimidated by its neoliberal spokespeople.

An important innovation was the formation of what became known as the Social Movements International Secretariat. Based on an initiative by the Brazilian labor union CUT and the landless movement MST (and by extension Via Campesina), many groups with leading roles in the worldwide fight against globalization, such as ATTAC and the French Peasants Confederation, the World March of Women, Euromarches against Unemployment, Jubilee South, Continental Social Alliance, 50 Years Is Enough!, and Focus on the Global South, discussed and approved the document "Porto Alegre Call for Mobilization" around a calendar of struggles, signed by hundreds of organizations and other entities. This text was a bruising critique of neoliberal globalization and a call for mass action during 2001 (see page 181). The protest against the FTAA and the mobilization during the G-8 Summit in Geneva were both highlighted in the text. This document, which also defined other struggles and protest initiatives for the year, pointed to a working convergence of all the initiatives against neoliberal globalization on the planet.

The forum exceeded everyone's initial expectations; it forced itself into the international media and contested the legitimacy of the meeting of businesspeople and government representatives in Davos. By presenting the World Social Forum as anti-Davos, as an affirmative and frontal counterposition to the World Economic Forum gathered in Switzerland, it received an even more prominent birth announcement. Simultaneously, the slogan "Another World Is Possible" became manifest in the open and deliberative exchange of experiences, in the debates about alternatives, and in the organization of the battles, so necessary to the global, heterogeneous movement. As Michael Löwy said in his presentation, "Davos and Porto Alegre represent two historical perspectives, two projects of civilization and two opposing social realities, antagonistic and irreconcilable."

The forum also succeeded because it was held in Porto Alegre and not in any other place. This city and the state of Rio Grande do Sul have been recognized as a point on the planet with solid social experience in formulating concrete alternatives to capitalist globalization (participatory budget making, battling genetically modified organisms, engaging in cooperative initiatives with the MST, and supporting the movement for free software, etc.). Additionally, the presence of the PT in the governments of Porto Alegre and Rio Grande do Sul ensured that great political weight and important resources would be directed to assuring the success of the forum and its accompanying activities.

It should also be noted that the efforts of French ATTAC and the groups involved with it, especially the journal *Le Monde Diplomatique*, were decisive in the international dissemination of the proposal for the forum. The activities of these groups were also key to the event itself. Totaling 130 people, the French delegation took on organizational tasks and initiatives, such as the live television debate "Porto Alegre—Davos," which contributed to the event's international repercussions.

The major media, particularly the Brazilian media, were initially prone to cast the event as a caricature, as a gathering of people left behind by the modernity represented by global-

---

Davos and Porto Alegre, Two Antagonistic Projects
Presentation of Michael Löwy at the first World Social Forum

Some well-intentioned souls have tried to reconcile Davos and Porto Alegre, arguing that both pursue the same objective: the humanization of the global economy. I am sorry to have to disagree with this point of view. For me—and I think that I am not alone in my thinking—Davos and Porto Alegre represent two historical perspectives, two projects of civilization and two opposing social realities, antagonistic and irreconcilable. The new century that began in January 2001 should opt for one of these two paths: a supposed "third way" does not exist.

Davos frequently uses the word "dialogue." The discussion via satellite between representatives of the two forums demonstrated the impossibility of dialogue: there is simply no common language. The people of the Forum of Porto Alegre live in this valley of tears, the spokespeople of Davos appear to have come from another planet, in which the free, unregulated market

ization. But they were won over by the sheer magnitude and profile of the forum, which not only made evident that Davos and neoliberalism represent deterioration for humanity but also demonstrated the existence of massive forces engaged in a search for alternatives. While the media were generally unable to acknowledge the political innovation the forum represented—instead mainly highlighting episodes such as the destruction, led by João Pedro Stedile and José Bové, of Monsanto's field of genetically modified soy and the peace protests by direct-action groups against a McDonald's—they could not hide the World Social Forum's size or importance.

---

brings happiness and prosperity for all, and neoliberal policies put an end to unemployment.

The economic and political elite of the globalized capitalist system is represented in Davos. There are the bankers, technocrats, businesspeople, speculators, officials and ministers who—except for a few exceptions—represent the interests of the financial oligarchy that dominates the global market. Despite their differences, they share a single idea, the same mercantile fetish, that which Leonardo Boff and Frei Betto call "market idolatry," a voracious idol that demands human sacrifices. They represent a system, neoliberal capitalism, intrinsically perverse, inhumane, responsible for the "economic horror" of unemployment and for monstrous social inequality. Just to cite one number: three North American billionaires, who are possibly at Davos, have a fortune that is equivalent to the Gross Domestic Product of 42 poor countries, where 600 million inhabitants live. This is a system responsible for neoliberal policies of structural adjustment, which sacrifice health and education budgets in

The forum finally reached its goals because it was ultimately transformed into something much larger and somewhat different from what was originally conceived, thus creating a new reality. Initially a meeting of 2,500 delegates from movements and social organizations, the World Social Forum finally reached around 4,000, offering a vast physical and political space, in which the different initiatives could coexist and also be added together, without becoming contradictory. The broadening of participation and the number of foci did not hurt, and in many ways helped, the movements and social organizations. The festive environment energized

---

order to pay off the external debt. A system responsible for the accelerated destruction of the environment by pollution of the air, land and sea, and for the greenhouse effect, which could produce, within a few years, an ecological catastrophe of unimaginable proportions. A system run by the law of the jungle: war of all against all, where the winner is the strongest, the most ferocious, the most merciless.

Faced with this, what does the first project of global counter-power, the World Social Forum of Porto Alegre, represent? It represents hope, a realistic and possible project for another world, of another local, national and worldwide economy directed at satisfying social necessities, respectful of the environment and ecological equilibrium; a realistic and possible project for another society, another civilization, based on the values of equality, solidarity, fraternity, cooperation, and mutual assistance. We are many, at this forum, who believe in socialism as the only authentic and radical alternative to the existing order of things; but we are united with our friends who do not

participants. Different types of initiatives could coexist and be organized in the forum, allowing the expressions of the resistance struggles' richness and all types of experiences in the construction of alternatives. Many initially unplanned parallel events enriched the World Social Forum without becoming confused with it, including the Parliamentarians Forum and the Youth Camp.

The parliamentarians met for the first time during an international conference on resistance to neoliberal globalization. Upon adopting the final declaration supporting the mobilizations, more than 210 parliamentarians from 29 coun-

---

share this opinion in the fight for concrete and immediate demands: the Tobin tax on speculative capital, abolition of the external debt, abolition of offshore tax havens, agrarian reform, moratoria on genetically modified organisms....

Now, this global counter-power can only be built, grow, sprout branches, leaves, flowers and fruits if it is rooted in concrete local reality, in local experiences of democratic management, but also in the struggle. I will mention just two examples of social movements, which are among the most actively committed to the project of this forum: the French Peasants Confederation (led by José Bové) and the Brazilian MST landless movement. These two only have the strength we know of because they are based in local experiences, local necessities and local struggles. They are radical movements, meaning, they go to the root of the problems. We were given a nice lesson in radicalism just a few days ago, by ripping out by the roots that which was rotten—in this case the multinational Monsanto's genetically modified plants.

tries committed to fight for the global movement's principal demands from within the elected institutions in which they participate and to form an international network to coordinate this action. The initiative, which was not tied down by complex diplomatic agreements among parties, enabled the flexible organization of social movements with political forces that could help in mobilizations by putting themselves at the service of the struggle. The political parties were, as such, present in the process, but in a measured manner, without taking center stage at the event.

A considerable number of participants at the forum were young people who identified with the new internationalism. Even though many of the direct-action groups that had been developing within the global movement did not go to Porto Alegre, the Intercontinental Youth Camp included a strong presence of the Brazilian sectors most engaged in struggle, such as delegations of students from the public universities in São Paulo (who had organized a long and victorious strike in 2000) and important participation of youth from the Mercosur trade bloc. Though the camp offered far from ideal conditions, as it was located in an area distant from the workshops and was partly permeated by the student movement dynamic,

---

To conclude: a certain neoliberal press, to confuse things, calls us "anti-globalization." This is a deliberate attempt at disinformation. This movement, this forum, is not anti-globalization: it is against *this capitalistic, neoliberal world,* unjust and inhumane, and it seeks *another world* of solidarity and fraternity. This new world is perhaps beginning in Porto Alegre in January 2001.

it enabled students and youth to attend the event, which was energized by their contagious enthusiasm and joyous and combative spirit.

The Camp of Indigenous Peoples from Rio Grande do Sul provided visibility to the victims of continuing modernization fueled by the world market, bringing to the scene an actor frequently ignored in these events.

The support of Porto Alegre's entertainment venues and services for the scheduling of large shows and artistic activities was indispensable to the extent that the forum was transformed into a huge event. This also had a political dimension, given that for the new movement, the alternatives that point to another world are also constructed from cultural expression and artistic work. The cultural activities were an important aspect of the first WSF, even if its political-cultural face was not emphasized.

The first WSF brought the worldwide movement against neoliberal globalization concretely to Brazil. Up to that point, the Brazilian Left's involvement with international initiatives had been relatively small, but the forum raised the awareness of a significant part of the democratic and public movement, principally on the necessity of fighting the FTAA. It was during the forum that the campaign for a public plebiscite on the FTAA was launched, which subsequently took place in September 2002. Many workshops and debates were held in which entities from the Continental Social Alliance and the Coalition of the Central Trade Unions of the Southern Cone played an active role, explaining the threat that the FTAA represented. The mobilizations in Buenos Aires and Quebec demonstrated the worth of the discussions held in Porto Alegre.

The forum played an important role in the organization of fights against globalization in South America and, principally, in the Southern Cone of the continent. More than seven hundred Argentines from various movements and political currents attended the forum. These activists did not have a history of cooperation in Argentina. For them, the forum represented a moment to meet, to work together, and to build a source of support for future common battles, as was witnessed during the 2001 crisis.

The forum had, in addition to this, a huge impact on the political dynamic in Rio Grande do Sul. From the moment of his election in 1998, Governor Olívio Dutra confronted a powerful opposition of local elites in a catastrophic economic situation, inherited from the earlier administration. His policies were blocked in the legislature and the judiciary, and he was experiencing difficulties with his social base. The forum enabled activists, for the first time, to shift the conflict with the local bourgeoisie toward a debate about the direction of society. The local right wing tried to question the forum and to protest against the Workers' Party governor. Soon, however, it had to retreat, put on the defensive by the event.

PLENARY SESSIONS AND WORKSHOPS

It is difficult to summarize the range of discussions held in the sixteen morning plenary sessions and the four hundred afternoon workshops. Various issues were addressed. A detailed evaluation is impossible here, but we can mention central debates, including an evaluation of the world economic situation; a discussion of the perspectives for deepening neoliberalism in the United States with George Bush Jr. in power; the rise in interimperialist rivalries, with Europe's search for more autonomy in relation to the United States; the limits for dismantling public services and the scope of private alternatives; the situation regarding international organizations (WTO, World Bank, IMF) and the possibility of their reform or destruction; the proposals to redefine the rules and mechanisms for international trade; the debate over canceling or negotiating Third World debt (and about the diverse situations within it); the fight for the Tobin tax and the discussion of the viability of its concrete application; the fight against regressive taxation mechanisms; the fight against offshore tax havens and corruption; the debate over development options for dependent countries; the mechanisms for economic solidarity; the fight against poverty; the role of cooperatives, local development, and possible social policies within the current framework; the fight against agribusiness and the use of genetically modified organisms; bioethics and the fight against patenting life; the fight against established intellectual property mechanisms; the diffusion of the use of free software; the right to information, democratization of communication, and social control of the media; participatory budgeting, forms of democratization of local power, the new forms of substantively exercising democracy; and worldwide organization of the fight against globalization.

These were just some of the most highlighted points of debate. The workshops introduced innumerable other important discussions about citizenship, education, higher learning, health, AIDS, transportation, energy, sanitation, water use, human rights, torture, gender, reproductive rights, the situation of Blacks and combating racism, indigenous people, physically challenged individuals, the situation of youths, children and adolescents, child labor, slave labor, prostitution, public security, immigration, refugees, opening borders, social security, the fight for a minimum wage, nutrition, fishing, urban reform and the situation of cities and housing, nationalism, regionalism, multiculturalism, the fight for peace, contesting tobacco use, combating land mines, new technologies, drugs, leadership training, community radio stations, art, utilization of direct-action techniques in the political fight, utopia, perspectives of social movements, the role of NGOs, consumer rights, journalism, Internet, independent media, liberation philosophy, philosophies for a new era, psychoanalysis and politics, ethics in politics, internationalism, socialism, regional unification, North–South relations, world governance, Latin America's situation, perspectives for its unification, memories of political repression on the continent, book launches, etc. It's worth noting that dozens of roundtables and speeches were held on some of these themes.

Any effort to structure these was, therefore, impractical, and raises a question that will continue to plague the organizers in subsequent forums. However, the forum did not propose to synchronize the events. The key point was opening debates to the entire gathering, and the dissemination of alternative proposals to neoliberalism and for the construction of another world.

LIMITATIONS AND PROBLEMS

The first WSF experienced a number of limitations and problems. Yet almost all of these could be forgiven because the event was the first of its kind and left a very positive impact when taken as a whole. The first was its still-tenuous internationalization. Despite the fact that much of the fight against neoliberal globalization was taking place in the English-speaking world and Asia, the forum was centered on delegations and movements from Latin America and Southern Europe (though the participation of around thirty delegations from Asia at the event was important). Also, the participation from Africa was negligible.

Second, the World Social Forum should not have had its format defined only by a Brazilian Organizing Committee. No uniquely national composition would provide the committee with the conditions to handle the complex problems presented by an event that had the ambition to be global, and more so in this case considering that none of the Brazilian organizations had, up to that point, played a central role in the international movement. This issue began to be addressed in June 2001, with the constitution of the International Council for the World Social Forum, which had some involvement in preparing the 2002 WSF and concretely participated in organizing the 2003 forum.

One problem of political direction generated a lot of noise among the social movements in the first WSF: the inclusion of two large general debates featuring personalities from Brazil (Lula, Olívio Dutra, Marta Suplicy, and Tarso Genro) and France (Jean-Pierre Chevènement and Guy Hascoët, who, as many social democrats from that country and present at the forum, were in the midst of full electoral campaigns). The debates were planned in one of the forum's main locations at PUC on the first day of discussions, the afternoon of January 26. The amount of program space given to these representatives of official politics in activities of social movements is always difficult to decide and frequently controversial. However, the greater visibility of these party leaders over social movement leaders was evident. This problem was compounded by the inclusion, among the speakers, of a clearly controversial figure, Chevènement, the French minister responsible for the repression of immigrants.

The question of whether to hold the next World Social Forum in Porto Alegre generated controversy. A majority of the Brazilian Organizing Committee did not want to decide at that moment where the second forum would be held. A compromise solution was found in the predawn hours before the closing plenary session. Concretely, it established that "a" forum would be held in Porto Alegre in 2002, on the same date as the World Economic Forum in Davos, opening the possibility of holding other forums in other locations.

For all those who were present in Porto Alegre, the birth of something new and very important was evident. Naomi Klein defined the forum as "A Fête for the End of the End of History," indicating that the alternatives of which "other world is possible" would be discussed again. While a large number of forum participants identified with some form of socialism, the majority was very distant from any type of tradition linked to the international socialists of the twentieth century. The forum, conceived as a broad convergence space for those who sought an alternative to neoliberal globalization, could prosper if it repeated the diversity of its components, maintained its political authority, strengthened ties with youth, and projected itself more successfully on an international level. But its alliances, mobilizations, and initiatives for its internal management still would have to be tested. Its perspectives were mixed up with those of the global movement from which it was born.

INTERNATIONAL COUNCIL AND CHARTER OF PRINCIPLES

With the success of the first World Social Forum and the decision to hold a second forum in Porto Alegre, the Brazilian Organizing Committee took two steps to reinforce the process. First, it systemized the forum experience in a Charter of Principles, and second, it convened a meeting of its international partners, with the objective of discussing the charter and using it as a basis to form an International Committee.

The formation of the International Committee was conceived in the initial WSF proposal: the general lines of the forum should be established by an international body that would reflect the global character of the fight against capitalist globalization. This definition was partially put into effect in a meeting held in São Paulo on June 10–11, 2001, in which more than sixty representatives of NGOs participated, including networks and social movements from Africa, Asia, Europe, and the Americas. Among the international participants were François Houtart of the World Forum for Alternatives, Nicola Bullard of Focus on the Global South, Njoki Njoroge Njehu of the 50 Years Is Enough Network, Bernard Cassen of ATTAC–France, Hector de la Cueva of the Continental Social Alliance, Eric Toussaint of the Committee for the Abolition of the Third World Debt (CADTM), Roberto Bissio of Social Watch, Beverly Keene of Jubilee South, and Victorio Agnoletto of the Genoa Social Forum that organized the 2001 protests against the G-8.

It was a partial creation because it was unclear, at first, whether the group that was formed was a committee or a council, given that the Brazilian Organizing Committee not only maintained its role as chief organizer but also defined policy. In practice, a gradual process was developed in which the inernational body would be seen as a council, but little by little it would share in the debates and responsibilities as an organizing committee, particularly after the second WSF.

The International Council (IC) established as its principal objective the internationalization of the WSF. It adopted the idea that the WSF was not only a happening, but also part of a participative process, and it accepted the proposal that the second forum should have an essentially deliberative character. The evaluation of the first WSF also pointed out some challenges, such as the incorporation of issues that were left aside or received little attention and the broadening of participation from other continents such as Africa and Asia.

At the São Paolo meeting, the IC defined its character, responsibilities, composition, and rules of operation. The document released by the group read:

> Creation of the IC reflects the concept of the WSF as a permanent, long-term process, designed to build an international movement to bring together alternatives to neoliberal thinking in favour of a new social order, one that will foster contact among a multiplicity and diversity of proposals.
>
> Accordingly, the IC will be set up as a permanent body that will give continuity to the WSF beyond 2002, to consolidate the process of taking the WSF to the world level. The Council will play a leading role in defining policy guidelines and the WSF's strategic directions. National Organizing Committees will serve as organizers and facilitators in tandem with the IC.

The discussion already affirmed the specific method of the forum, and as a result:

> The IC must be a place of ongoing, open dialogue and interlinking with other social movements and struggles. It will not be an authority in a power structure, and will not have mechanisms for disputing representation, nor for voting. Although the IC must have a balanced make-up in terms of regional and sectorial diversity, it will not be a bureaucratic structure with any claim to representing world civil society. The representativity of the IC will result from its ability to take the WSF to the world level, and to give it roots, organicity and continuity.

It recognized the limitations, in that moment, of the forum process and the IC by expressing:

> The IC consists of a basic core wherein regional imbalances still exist (sparse participation by Africa, Asia and the Arab world), as well as sectorial ones (young people, Blacks, among others), which must be eliminated. The Council believes that confronting these imbalances and gaps must be seen as a goal to be attained by means of consultation, for which regions and groups require time.

In this spirit, the IC scheduled its next two meetings: the first in Dakar, Senegal, in October 2001, and then another in Porto Alegre before the beginning of the second WSF.

The International Council also approved a reformulation of the Charter of Principles that the Organizing Committee had adopted two months earlier. The Charter of Principles defined the WSF as "an open meeting place," which did not mean an organization, entity, institution, or network. The forum is politically delineated as a space of "groups and movements of civil society opposed to neoliberalism and to domination of the world by capital and any form of imperialism." Its proposals "stand in opposition to a process of globalization commanded by the large multinational corporations and by the governments and international institutions at the service of those corporations' interests, with the complicity of national governments."

World Social Forum events have a nondeliberative character for the WSF as a body. This frequently questioned procedural point is based on the idea that the WSF "does not constitute a locus of power to be disputed by the participants in its meetings," and no one "will be authorized, on behalf of any of the editions of the Forum, to express positions claiming to be those of all its participants. The participants ... shall not be called on to take decisions as a body, whether by vote or by acclamation." The Charter of Principles states, however, that "organizations or groups of organizations that participate in the Forum meetings must be assured the right ... to deliberate on declarations or actions they may decide on," and which the Forum will disseminate widely. The Forum held no assemblies in which it spoke, made decisions on its behalf, or approved resolutions, which could have restricted any sector participating in it.

The WSF "will always be a forum open to pluralism and to the diversity of activities and ways of engaging." The forum "brings together and interlinks only organizations and movements of civil society from all the countries in the world." The Charter of Principles considers pluralism a source of richness and strength. The forum will coexist with contradictions and will always be marked by conflicting opinions among the organizations and movements whose positions lie within the bounds of the Charter of Principles. However, it is established that "neither party representations nor military organizations shall participate in the Forum." This generic formulation was finally adopted after a debate around an initial proposal to reject the use of violence in politics.

Different motives can be identified for not allowing political parties to participate as organizers of the World Social Forum, but one that stands out is the framework that had been characterized in many debates within the forum of the crisis of political representation of the Left. This is evident as much in the limits confronted by international initiatives of parties, such as the São Paulo Forum formed in 1990 to bring together the leftist parties in Latin America, which were frequently transformed into international summits, as in the distant relationships that many of these parties have with the new movement that has emerged in recent years in the fight against neoliberalism. The global movement has had frequent difficulties in relating to the parties identified as representing the status quo.

But the Charter of Principles does assert, "Government leaders and members of legislatures who accept the commitments of this Charter may be invited to participate in a personal capacity." The invitation to parliamentarians and government leaders is, as such, sent as a matter of political courtesy to allow them to decide if they want to attend the WSF based on their relationship to the movement and its battles. Beyond this, what is important for the activities promoted collectively by the organizers is that the WSF is open and does not operate on the basis of invitations. It provides the conditions necessary for all those interested in promoting their activities to be able to do so, under whatever name (workshops, seminars, meetings, forums, etc.).

It is precisely working on this terrain that the World Parliamentary Forum and the Forum of Local Authorities dialogued with the WSF and its participants. The International Council organized these as autonomous events with the same status as the other seminars. A Parliamentary Committee took responsibility for organizing the first and the Porto Alegre city government took responsibility for organizing the second. There is a collaborative relationship and respect for the autonomous spaces on the part of both the forum and the parliamentarians and local government leaders.

The Charter of Principles acts as a "constitution" and political boundary for the World Social Forum process. The events that began to be promoted around the world and under the name World Social Forum should be regarded as part of the process supported by the IC and respected within the definitions established in its charter. Some themes, such as relationships with governments, multilateral institutions, armed organizations, and political parties, reemerge periodically as points of debate, but the terms of the Charter of Principles have, until now, always been upheld. The charter provides that the internationalization of the WSF does not signify, from a political point of view, its fragmentation.

CHAPTER FOUR

The Forum as a Global Movement Convergence Space

The year 2001 was notable. After the first World Social Forum in January, the ascending curve of mobilizations continued to develop until it reached its climax during the demonstrations in Genoa against the G-8 meeting. The global institutions' crisis of legitimacy reached its apex. The internationalist movement expressed a clear rejection, by a substantial part of civil society, of neoliberal globalization. The year was also marked by the September 11 terrorist attacks and the offensive launched by the new right-wing U.S. government on national and international terrain, developing a policy to restrict civil liberties and for a profound militarization in international affairs. At the end of the year, a vast coalition of countries went to war against the fundamentalist Taliban government in Afghanistan. Many journalists commented then that the global movement had lost its momentum and would be marginalized within the new political scene. It was at this time that the WSF revealed its potential as a convergence space for all resistances.

THE SECOND WORLD SOCIAL FORUM

The second World Social Forum, from January 31 to February 5, 2002, represented a significant moment for the global movement. The first large event by the movement against neoliberalism following September 11, the second WSF attested to the fact that the "war against terrorism" by Bush and his allies, which attempted to criminalize all opposition to the system, did not break the momentum of the protests. The imperial war and the attempt to establish a planetary state of siege moved to the center of world politics, posing new problems and demanding answers. However, the tone of Porto Alegre was set not by the North American agenda but by the deepening criticism of neoliberal globalization, the movement's solidarity ties, and the constructive forces of a new global agenda. This would echo over the following months, for example, in the gigantic protests in Barcelona and Rome.

In an extremely dynamic assembly, the forum could also bring together, a few months after the imperial offensive was launched, the huge mobilizing energies liberated by the popular revolt against neoliberalism in Argentina, an exemplary case of the destruction of a country by the tyranny of markets, a synthesis of "Davos wisdom," as Samuel Pinheiro Guimarães said.* The forum could also debate, as some delegates from English-speaking countries highlighted, the energy company Enron's bankruptcy in the United States as an unequivocal demonstration of corporate despotism over citizens.

---

* Samuel Pinheiro Guimarães is vice chancellor of Brazil. As a former ambassador and foreign policy expert, he is a critic of neoliberal globalization and free-trade policies that harm developing countries.

The second forum witnessed the movement's expansion and internationalization, and the advance of an internationalist political consciousness against neoliberalism, contributing to a qualitative leap in its consolidation in a more hostile political environment.

By the numbers it drew, the WSF 2002 was a huge success, exceeding sixty thousand participants, triple the attendance in 2001. More than 53,000 people were registered at the forum (35,000 observers; 15,000 delegates; and 3,000 journalists) and 11,000 in the Youth Camp. More important, the number of delegates jumped from four thousand to fifteen thousand, representing around five thousand organizations, almost half from abroad. The data attest to the relationship of the forum with the decisive battles against neoliberalism. Almost one thousand Italians were present, testifying to the impact of the Genoa Social Forum and the July mobilization against the G-8. A similar number of Argentines participated, representing the militancy that led the December 2001 *cacerolazos* (mass pot-banging demonstrations). The participation of Asian and African delegations also increased, although these regions were still underrepresented, as did the number of delegations from the United States, which was very small at the earlier forum.

There was an impressive change in the forum's composition: an enormous growth of the Youth Camp and its internationalization demonstrated the global movement's increasing appeal to the new generation of the political Left that was emerging. Eleven thousand people who were enrolled had their credentials suspended in a frustrated attempt to stop more people from camping in Harmony Park. In a new example of how to debate and organize, the youth confronted the challenge of running a real city with enormous structural problems. Around 15,000 youths lived a five-day experience of radical liberty, as opposed to conservatism, passivity, alienation, and consumerism. They also challenged a certain more moderate and/or bureaucratic trend present inside the forum and among some youth organizations. Another significant change was the higher participation of wageworkers, few of whom had been present at the earlier forum. They were now represented in force by the main international unions.

In its assemblage, the second forum legitimized the WSF as a space in which the global movement could meet; dialogue; establish trusting relationships among the participants; learn from different experiences, partnerships, and reflections; encounter support in multiple struggles; and consolidate a common mobilization agenda. In this way, a space for positive expression of diversity, a source of the movement's strength and richness, was created. This allowed different political cultures to live together, and a common identity was forged on the horizon of shared experiences in a climate of mutual respect. The global movement generalized the method of organizing the forum: preserving the individual identities of its parts but making it possible for them to join together into a large, open movement to which everyone could contribute—plural from a political and ideological point of view but no less committed to the fights against exploitation, injustice, and oppression and for the search for liberty, justice, equality, and solidarity.

EXPRESSION OF DIVERSITY, CONVERGENCES, AND INTERNATIONALIZATION

A general understanding of the need for the forum as a systematic, global meeting place ended up prevailing at the third meeting of the International Council on January 28–29, 2002. The internationalization of the WSF would be promoted by holding various regional and continental forums at the end of 2002, while guaranteeing that a "centralized" third WSF would be held in Porto Alegre in January 2003 and a fourth would be held at the same time in 2004, in an as yet undetermined location. The International Council also decided to strengthen its structure during 2002.

> The second WSF was a practical space for constructing convergences. The organizing initiatives presented there were consolidated, in practice, into a global mobilization calendar for the following two years, establishing a common horizon for the multiple battles. The WSF organized delegation meetings by continent, reinforcing the dynamic that directed regional and continental forums. It gave continuity to the international organization of social movements—initiated even before the first WSF and reinforced by a worldwide meeting in August 2001 in Mexico, which launched in this forum a second call for mobilizations titled "Resistance Against Neoliberalism, Militarism and War: For Peace and Social Justice." (See page 187.)

The Intercontinental Youth Camp, the "Laboratory for Global Resistance," launched the project Intergalactika—a "contagion" space for diverse movements and mobilizations involving the new political generation that was emerging on a world scale. It also defined an effort to reclaim May 1 as a "Day of Struggle and Global Resistance" from the bureaucratic labor federations and political parties that had come to dominate protests on this date.

The forum provided for political and organizational leaps in the campaigns against the FTAA, the WTO, the patenting of life, and the dissemination of genetically modified organisms. It also boosted campaigns for the abolition of dependent countries' external debt and for taxation of international financial transactions. It afforded Argentine delegates an opportunity for discussions that contributed to their reflection on the process under way in their country. It allowed for debate on the question of peace with social justice in the general militarization of international affairs. This was accomplished by means of direct links with the January–February 2002 demonstrations against Davos in New York, through which the global movement in the United States regained its initiative; through the seminar "A World Without War Is Possible," which discussed alternatives to overcome the conflicts in Chiapas, Spain's Basque country, Colombia, and Palestine; and through the "World Public Assembly for Participatory Budgeting with War Spending" (which surpasses $800 billion annually!). This assembly was a teach-in that concretely showed that it is possible to eliminate the great evils that plague humanity. It provided for a discussion of socialism in an activity promoted by Via Campesina, the seminar "Socialism, the Hopeful Alternative." It also cosponsored various like-minded conferences: the World Forum of Local Authorities, the Preparatory Meeting for the Rio+10 Conference about the environment, and the World Judges Forum.

The second WSF provided meeting spaces and support for different sectors: in addition to youth and the world of work, the Black movement, the women's movement, indigenous peoples' movements, and the movement for free sexual orientation appeared at the forum and developed their initiatives. Support for the ideas of sustainable development, participatory democracy, defense of common goods such as public health care and education, and decommercialization of the world permeated the assemblage of debates. And two huge street demonstrations—the first, "Against War and for Peace, Another World Is Possible," on January 31, and the second, "March against the FTAA," on February 4—reinforced the activist tone of the WSF.

The decision by the first WSF and the Charter of Principles not to debate about the structure of the forum or to take forum-wide votes on resolutions proved correct. More open and fruitful discussions were permitted, power struggles reduced, and the ability of those who wished to organize was not impeded. It was a particularly effective method for the construction of a new global agenda in a framework of ideological and organizational diversity, which must bring together a wide array of sometimes very unequal experiences, without prioritizing one over the others, while maintaining a strong educational character. A good part of the vitality of the forum stemmed from the close, but not always easy, proximity of social movements directly engaged in fighting neoliberal globalization, on one hand, with the central unions, NGOs, and cooperative agencies, on the other. The WSF united without commanding and preserved ideological and organizational diversity—a practice that is still strange for a large part of the Left.

TENSIONS WITH PARTIES AND PARLIAMENTARIANS

The forum's success reverberated as a victory for the governments of the state of Rio Grande do Sul and the city administration of Porto Alegre, both of which offered indispensable political and material support, guaranteeing, together with a vast network of local militants, a democratic and productive climate for all the activities. Support for the WSF continued to provide "movement" credentials to the Workers' Party (PT) governments of the city and state, reinforcing the image of the PT as a party close to the social movements and not considered by a large part of them to be the enemy.

A complex issue, whose full weight was expressed in this second forum, was the relationship between social movements and political parties. The World Parliamentary Forum, which was attended by eight hundred parliamentarians from forty countries, constituted a productive space for different parties and parliamentarians seeking to identify with the WSF process. At this forum, the International Parliamentary Network was set up. But the process was contradictory. The global movement favored the reconstruction of a new anti-imperialist, anticapitalist Left with the political parties attuned to the movement rather than a Left where the movements would be integrated into the parties and governments, many of which are committed to neoliberal policies. This structural contradiction was expressed in the discussion about whether the parliamentary forum should issue an explicit condemnation of the war against Afghanistan. The parliamentary forum did resolve to issue such a condemnation. This debate reinforced the need, in the current context, to maintain the World Parliamentary Forum and other initiatives of this type, such as the Local Authorities Forum, as autonomous and delineated from the WSF—an ambiguous but effective means of balancing, at that moment, this tense and delicate relationship.

To the extent that the forum became stronger and gained legitimacy and political and moral authority, it began to suffer pressure from sectors linked to the international order (neoliberal governments, social-liberal currents, international organs), which wanted visibility and leading roles in the WSF, even in contradiction to the agreements in the Charter of Principles. This was the case with the vice president of the World Bank, who attended the Local Authorities Forum, held immediately before the WSF, and tried through various means to be invited to the WSF. The Belgian prime minister, called "Baby Thatcher" in his country, invited himself to the forum. Both of these initiatives were, for their symbolism, refused by the Brazilian Organizing Committee and the International Council, which rejected the attempts to dilute the counterposition of Davos and Porto Alegre and to empty the WSF of the "Spirit of Seattle."

The sensation of fragmentation and dispersion resulting from the growth of the forum expressed a very positive phenomenon: the WSF is a horizontal construction of innumerable collective actors. The convergence process of the global movement for participation, social justice, and solidarity was provided around concrete and delineated themes, emphasized in the WSF 2002 conferences. However, the need to organize around fundamental issues of world politics was evident as much in the general diagnosis of how the current world system of power operates as in what could be an alternative world order able to make viable the proposals that the WSF disseminated.

Other problems—such as the disproportionate presence of Western European and North American white men in prominent positions in almost all of the activities, the difficulty of establishing a more collectively negotiated definition of the spaces, the initiation of decentralization in this WSF in Porto Alegre without support or previous preparation for this, and the obvious difficulties in organizing an event of this magnitude—were expressed. However, none of these questions compromised the forum's political significance.

A PROTEST MAP

The Brazilian Organizing Committee, the International Council, and the international networks prepared twenty-seven conferences for the second WSF. They were grouped around four axes defined in the earlier forum: the production of wealth and social reproduction, access to wealth and sustainability, the affirmation of civil society and public spaces, and political and ethical power in the new society. There was, this time, a methodology of preparing documents, synthesizing discussions, and systematizing the proposals, resulting in an enormous repertory of diagnoses and ideas. A mapping of the problems, analyses, and alternatives was initiated, enabling an important leap forward in the formulation and gradual construction of an alternative program for the global movement. Unfortunately, the same focus was not provided for the rest of the forum activities: it was possible to recover only a small part of the discussions held in the approximately seven hundred workshops and one hundred seminars.

But innumerable proposals can be highlighted, even in their very partial form. They confirm the World Social Forum as a most important space for the development of a new global agenda. We will mention some of them, summarized by Thomas Ponniah,* who worked voluntarily on the WSF 2002 report.

- *Abolition of poor countries' external debt:* Popularized by Jubilee South and CADTM, this proposal seeks to free up resources, today drained from dependent economies by the international financial system, and to permit their utilization to combat poverty and promote development. A variety of political strategies, such as alliances with debtor countries and pressure on creditor country governments, has been debated.

- *Controls on international financial capital and taxation for wealth redistribution and development financing:* ATTAC popularized the Tobin tax proposal, an international tax on the circulation of speculative capital. The control of the origin and objectives in financial operations and the institution of obligatory reserve deposits and guarantees would also substantially decrease money-laundering and offshore "bankers' paradises."

- *Moratorium on the WTO to reorient international trade:* The existing movements seek sovereign and altruistic protectionism and oppose the imposed liberalization of trade, which deepens inequalities. This demands a revision of a majority of the agreements presently adopted by the WTO. Regarding the future of the institution, there is divergence over whether a reformed WTO should remain or whether the WTO should simply be abolished. Special attention is given in this discussion to the elimination of intellectual property rights incorporated in the treaty that forms the WTO and in the patent legislation in effect today. In the area of information technology, the free software movement stimulates the demand for intellectual property rights.

- *Public control of transnational companies:* A variety of multinational observers and campaigns propose international legislation that demands of multinational companies an end to

---

* For more discussion on these points, see William F. Fisher and Thomas Ponniah, eds., *Another World Is Possible* (London and New York: Zed Press, 2003).

the secrecy under which they operate and responsibility for their actions, particularly in the areas of labor rights and the environment. These companies should be submitted to periodic external audits by credible institutions.

- *Defense of labor rights:* Unions have worked for decades to assure compliance with labor and union rights established by the ILO (International Labor Organization) and propose the creation of parliamentary groups to protect these rights. The unions in the South also propose a system of global collective bargaining and the organization of international campaigns to protect workers in poor countries. Some movements advocate boycotts of transnational corporations that violate different types of rights.

- *Development of a solidarity economy sector:* A vast group of movements defend the promotion, from today onward, of an economic sector based on cooperatives and associations that operate outside the logic of the free market. For some this can be the embryo of a social sector capable of complementing, limiting, or substituting, depending on the perspective, the capitalistic economy.

- *Environmental reconstruction and sustainable development:* Innumerable organizations and environmental movements around the world defend a development model based on sustainability through compliance with international agreements that limit the greenhouse effect; implement alternative energy sources; install clean production systems; extend ecological agriculture; modify consumption forms, principally in rich countries; and recognize the environmental debt. The question of managing the use of potable water has a great urgency, given the crises that already impact many populations. In its totality, this issue calls for another development model based on the recognition of the planet's finite resources and on solidarity with future generations.

- *Creation and extension of public and universal health and education systems:* Popular movements worldwide defend these systems, demanding guarantees of public resources and their use for this objective, combating privatization of these services, and demanding the effective right of access to necessary medications (reviewing the patent system in effect, as is the case with medications against AIDS). In education, the model of public education should favor equality and social integration, disseminating democratic values, solidarity, and ecology and combating intolerance and discrimination.

- *Food sovereignty:* Movements such as Via Campesina demand the strengthening of agricultural cooperatives directed at satisfying national necessities and for the diversification of food resources in each country; national market protection; the abolition of agricultural product subsidies in Northern countries, which strangle Southern countries' production in the international market; and a moratorium on the commercial use of genetically modified organisms, which are being used in a large part of the world by large agribusiness transnationals for the destruction of family agricultural production.

- *Democratization of mass communication outlets:* Innumerable entities seek to establish social control over the corporate media and emphasize this as a precondition, in the current world, to achieving a right to information, education, and the possibility of citizens' participation, as well as the preservation of peoples' cultural identities.

- *Defense of peoples' identities:* Guarantees of the rights of national minorities and indigenous peoples and the promotion of their cultures.

- *Rights of immigrants and combating the trafficking of people:* Alteration of restrictive legislation that makes tens of millions of workers throughout the world illegal, guaranteeing free circulation of people and unification of families.

- *Disarmament:* Proposals range from the reduction of up to 3 percent of the costs of arms in countries worldwide to make way for the creation of a fund to finance peace and development projects, to the international control of arms trade.

- *Integral human rights:* The understanding of a growing group of movements is that the fight on this issue should be for integrity and universality of human rights, which should not be reduced only to civil and political rights, and demand the recognition of economic, social, cultural, and environmental rights.

- *New international institutions for global governance:* Short-term reforms in the World Bank, IMF, and WTO, according to some, seeking to impose greater transparency and democracy in their internal functioning. Others defend their abolition. In all cases, the demand for control mechanisms by civil society organizations and parliaments is defended.

These examples do not exhaust all possible topics, but they are an indication of the wealth of alternatives that are being debated in social forums worldwide and in Porto Alegre in 2002.

THE FORUM AS A GLOBAL EVENT: THE THIRD WORLD SOCIAL FORUM

Following the substantial political impact of the second WSF, preparation for the third became an enormous challenge. With the effective functioning of the International Council (IC), the discussions about the organization of WSF 2003 were shared between the IC and the Organizing Committee. An intense schedule of meetings was established, with the IC meeting three times between the two forums—in Barcelona, Bangkok, and Florence—in addition to the regular meeting immediately before the WSF. International working groups participated in preparing the conferences, panels, and a new type of activity called "dialogue and controversy roundtables" between civil society, on one side, and political parties, governments, and multilateral institutions, on the other.

This preparation for the forum took place during a time of profound change in the international scene, including the deepening economic crisis and, principally, the militarization of international affairs between the United States and other countries. The thematic forums of Argentina and Palestine and the regional forums in Europe and Asia grasped this change in the agenda and facilitated the political preparation of Porto Alegre 2003.

When the third World Social Forum met, January 23–28, 2003, it was a great victory for the movement with which it identified. The Forum achieved greater visibility than the earlier ones, attracting media from around the world and pushing Davos into the background. As a global event for the worldwide media, the forum had arrived.

Porto Alegre 2003 grew greatly on the quantitative front. The number of participants increased from 60,000 to around 100,000: 20,763 delegates from 130 countries; 4,094 credentialed journalists; and 25,000 campers in the Youth Camp were registered on the WSF's site. The activities multiplied: almost seventeen hundred workshops and seminars, thirty-one panels, eleven conferences, four dialogue and controversy roundtables (some attracting forty thousand people), twenty-one testimonials, and two enormous marches, one each at the opening and closing of the forum.

Unlike in previous years, WSF 2003 activities were widely dispersed throughout the city of Porto Alegre. Events took place in three main venues: the Gigantinho Stadium, the Pontifical Catholic University (PUC) campus, and the port storage facilities. Huge conferences and dialogue-and- controversy roundtables were held in the Gigantinho Stadium, panels were held at the port, and PUC hosted the workshops and seminars organized by attendees.

The panels (called "conferences" in 2001 and 2002) established an environment of debate and discussion on proposals for the civil society networks and organizations. The panels were organized by the WSF Secretariat, along with the International Council, divided by working groups around five thematic points (different from the four themes of earlier years): democratic and sustainable development; principles and values, human rights, diversity, and equality; media, culture, and counterhegemony; political power, civil society, and democracy; and democratic world order, combating militarization, and promoting peace. Six panels (with the exception of the first point, which had seven) appeared under each theme, for a total of thirty-one panels. Also in 2003, a moment on the final day of panel presentations was reserved for a synthesis of the proposals debated throughout the three earlier days. The preparation of WSF activities was more internationalized, involving the International Council in the definition of methodology and themes, and resulting in the inclusion of new themes. This also made possible the internationalization of participants in expositions and conferences.

The large conferences in the afternoons and the dialogue-and-controversy roundtables in the mornings made Gigantinho into a huge gathering place for the WSF. These events, featuring well-known personalities, were organized for an audience made up of people who were not activists affiliated with any organization involved in self-organized activities. Public attendance reached around twenty thousand people on all days, increasing to forty thousand for the conferences about "peace and values," and at the closing, "Confronting Empire," with Noam Chomsky and Arundhati Roy.

The 21 testimonials and 1,286 activities autonomously organized by the delegates were concentrated on the PUC campus. The autonomously organized activities addressed the most diverse themes. Some even organized themselves into a program of dozens of meetings, such as the discussions under the title "Life After Capitalism" promoted by ZNet.

The WSF 2003 also gave more prominence to cultural programming. Since a central theme of the forum focused on "media, culture, and counterhegemony," organizing this part of the program fell to a working group of the Brazilian Organizing Committee that mobilized local cultural movements. The cultural program, including shows, expositions, film screenings, and theater presentations, was intense.

In addition to the variety of activities held under the umbrella of the World Social Forum, diverse parallel events, such as the World Labor Forum, the World Choral Forum, the World Parliamentary Forum, the Little World Social Forum for children, the Sexual Diversity Forum, the Local Authorities Forum, the World Education Forum, and the World Judges Forum, also took place.

All this did not happen without problems, however. With the enormous growth of the WSF and the reduction of government support as a result of the electoral defeat of the Workers' Party in Rio Grande do Sul, managing the event became more difficult. Important organizational problems occurred, particularly in the allocation of workshops and the housing of participants in Porto Alegre. Difficulties accommodating the tremendous size and scheduling of all the practically simultaneous activities prompted criticism from participants and organizers that would be incorporated into the planning of the fourth WSF in Mumbai, India.

PORTO ALEGRE FACES ARMED GLOBALIZATION

Beyond considerations of its size, diversity, and impact, the third WSF should be analyzed politically as a space and a moment in which the agenda for the struggle against neoliberalism definitively linked up with an agenda to fight militarization and imperialism.

We are increasingly confronted with, as Claude Sefarti said, "armed globalization," and it was against this that Porto Alegre debated alternatives. In the second WSF, even following September 11 and the attack on Afghanistan, the agenda of activities proposed by the organizers only peripherally addressed the question of war and militarization. The question of the structure of world political domination was still, to a large extent, discussed in terms of the multilateralism of the 1990s. Only a theoretical discussion titled "Empire or Imperialism," owing to the publication of the book *Empire,* by Michael Hardt and Antonio Negri, made it to a prominent spot on the program. Now, mobilizing against war and empire had become a central question of the gathering and a point of debate in the European Social Forum and the Asian Social Forum. This showed that the issue of war and empire was being absorbed into the agenda of the countless social movements that oppose neoliberal globalization. This project was most evidently problematic in the United States, but to the extent to which the war preparations against Iraq advanced in the second half of 2002, the antiwar movement was able to reestablish some dialogue with unions and environmental and other movements. The economic role of war in the context of recession; a new imperial domination strategy adopted by the dominant class in the United States; the resurgence of conflicts between the leading imperial powers such as the United States and the European Union; and the "state of siege" mentality that was emerging (along with the disregard for internationally recognized human rights) from the Bush doctrine began to figure prominently in the debates.

In the immediate context of preparing for the third WSF, the IC and the Brazilian social movements had an important role in focusing the agenda around this point. The opening panel was about the fight against militarization and the war; the closing was about confronting imperial domination. These were also the themes of the opening and closing marches organized by local organizations in Rio Grande do Sul. The forum probably made an important contribution in promoting the proposal, born in Florence, to organize a worldwide day of protest against the war on February 15, 2003. This reverberated enormously throughout the world.

This entire process did not resolve the complex problems of organizing between "the social" and "the strictly political" (the empire and the war), but it undoubtedly expressed the global movement's greater political maturity. This relationship between the social and the political was also at the heart of another featured (and very controversial) point at the third WSF: the presence of government representatives. In a context of the profound crises of neoliberalism in South American countries, the left alternatives had grown throughout 2002, with the failure of the anti-Chávez coup in Venezuela during the period immediately before the forum; the presidential candidacy of Evo Morales in Bolivia; and the electoral victories of Lucio Gutierrez in Ecuador and, principally, of Lula in Brazil.

The presence of Lula (invited by the WSF organizers) and Hugo Chávez (for another activity, autonomous of the forum) were remarkable moments of the third WSF. Lula and Chávez attended, drawn to the political pole of attraction that the forum had come to represent. However, their presence as government leaders imposed a new type of relationship between the movements meeting at the WSF and government leaders.

Lula's presence, which in principle should have had a more diplomatic character (as the host government identified with the forum), became very controversial with his decision to go from Porto Alegre to Davos, where he would participate in the World Economic Forum. The presence of the government leaders led Naomi Klein to characterize the third WSF as the "Forum of Great Men," which was, for her, a backward step from the earlier forums. This comment was a one-sided criticism, which ignored the vast web of horizontal initiatives that were presented there and that continued to provide the tone of the WSF 2003; however, it did express an important feeling present in the WSF that year.

What undoubtedly is highlighted in the evaluation of the third WSF is that political debate, in the classical sense of the term, was much more integrated into the themes and perspectives of the discussions. The relationships between the social and the political implied, however, tensions and contradictions, which emerged openly in 2003 and will continue to exist in the WSF process.

CHAPTER FIVE

Globalization and the Future of The World Social Forum

Immediately before the second WSF, on January 28–29, 2002, the International Council (IC) met to define the forum's future perspectives. At a third meeting of the IC, it was clear that the WSF 2002 would be a huge success, but the Brazilian Organizing Committee still did not have a common vision of the continuity of the process. The question was put very openly to debate. After a long and heated discussion, the IC reached a resolution that since then has directed the World Social Forum process. It was summarized at the time in the following terms:

> The meeting affirmed the idea that the WSF, much more than an event, was consolidating as a process and an open movement, which was internationalizing and creating roots on all continents. The composition of the International Council demonstrates the broadening of social forces, which all over the planet are committed to a permanent WSF.
>
> The International Council has determined that the organization of an annual and centralized WSF is fundamental for the meeting and organization of the multiple forces that op-

pose neoliberal globalization. Additionally, the event itself has a public impact important for the movement's dynamism. Finally, the International Council considers that an effective internationalization of the WSF demands mobilization growth in regions in order to broaden participation on all continents.

Considering this framework, the International Council decided the following:

1. In the second semester in different parts of the world, continental and regional versions of the World Social Forum will be held;
2. We will again hold the third World Social Forum in Porto Alegre and on the same date as the World Economic Forum;
3. The WSF International Council will play a key role in organizing the dynamics of the regional and continental forums and the centralized World Social Forum. This will be the main issue of the Council meeting scheduled for April 28–30, 2002.

At the next IC meeting in Barcelona in April, a new element was added to this proposal: the possibility of holding not only regional forums, but also thematic ones—addressing controversial issues of the international situation with a universal appeal. This perspective was effectively implemented during 2002. The forum became a global process. In a period in which the shock waves of a new imperial offensive resonated worldwide, a number of social forums were organized. Many of these forums were autonomous initiatives of local organizations or national forums, about which the IC and Secretariat frequently became aware only after the events had occurred. However, some forums were organized in conjunction with the global process, giving them a greater ability to attract participants and to have a political impact.

THE PROCESS OF WSF INTERNATIONALIZATION

The first regional forum had taken place even before the process was defined: the African Social Forum met in Bamako, the capital of Mali, in December 2001. With the NGO ENDA acting as lead organizer, it brought together 250 representatives of organizations and movements on the continent.

The event that, according to the open-activity method of the WSF, inaugurated a new phase was the thematic forum proposed in the Barcelona meeting and rapidly organized by the Argentine entities that were members of the IC—CLASCO, Dialogue 2000–Jubilee South, the Argentine Workers Central (CTA), and the Latin American Association of Small and Medium-Sized Enterprises (ALAMPYME). Using the Argentine upheavals of December 19–20, 2001, as a focus, the thematic forum "The Crisis of Neoliberalism in Argentina and the Global Movement's Challenges" was organized. Held in Buenos Aires August 22–25, 2002, it drew more than ten thousand participants and, for the first time, created a convergence space for the fragmented Left of that country. It was a moment of coming together for the *piquetero* protesters, the militants of popular assemblies and their supporters, and innumerable leftist currents, involving more than six hundred social organizations. A march of thirty thousand people, led by the indigenous Bolivian leader Evo Morales, opened the forum. Actions against the FTAA and the militarization of Latin America were coordinated there. Alternatives to the national crisis were debated, and wide visibility to the indigenous issue in the country (normally ignored by the Left) was achieved. In addition, a warning of the danger of criminalizing social protests was raised. Unfortunately, despite the large impact of this initiative, the forum was unable to play a more long-term role in unifying the Argentine popular movement, which continued to rely on its traditional political culture.

The European Social Forum (ESF) harnessed the energy that was released in the protests against the G-8 meeting in Genoa in July 2001, the global movement's largest protest to that point. The enormous Italian delegation that attended the second WSF in Porto Alegre organized itself with the other representatives of European organizations (principally French) and agreed to hold the ESF 2002 in Italy, and the ESF 2003 in France. Florence, governed by a progressive regional and municipal government, was chosen to host the event. However, preparations for the ESF were the source of a difficult political battle in Italy between the Left and the Berlusconi government, which tried to block it. This served to reinforce the forum's political impact. As such, when the forum met November 6–9, 2002, in beautiful Fortezza da Basso exhibition hall, sixty thousand participants attended. (This was the same number of people at the second WSF, although at its first meeting, the Italian Organizing Committee had expected five thousand participants.)

The ESF had a gigantic political impact, in part because of the specific conditions of the Italian situation—marked since Genoa by its strong political polarization between the mass social movements and the rightist government—but also because, for the first time, it began to bring together the European resistances against neoliberalism and the war. More than 3,000 French were present, as were delegations of around 1,500 from Greece, Spain, the United Kingdom, and Germany; 300 Hungarians; 150 Poles; and 70 Russians. The forum was the moment of affirmation of a new political generation, which for the first time appeared as the majority in an event of this type, facing a continental Left that had up to that point been largely made up of the 1968 generation.

The ESF introduced a new process to the WSF, a model of organizing in which all preparatory meetings (which were held in different countries on the continent) were open to the more than five hundred organizations that wanted to participate. This dynamic is slower because it implies a dialogue, which is sometimes difficult. As a result, however, it creates more commitment from all involved. In the absence of organizational bodies that had uncontestable legitimacy to make the necessary decisions about the activities to be organized by the event's promoters, and with spaces set aside for autonomous organization of activities, this open process is indispensable. Even so, forum organizers had to confront enormous organizing problems, owing to the fact that the number of participants was three times higher than expected. Many of the activities planned to be held outside the convention center (particularly the workshops distributed around the city) did not occur, repeating on a large scale the problem that had been observed in Porto Alegre in 2002 and that would be more pronounced in 2003.

The balance sheet of the ESF was very positive. Different reports of the ESF spoke of the birth of a European social movement, which began to make possible the contesting of issues in the European Union consolidation process. The ESF organized a mass protest of more than half a million people on

Saturday, November 9. At that protest, the fight against the imperial war—the war in Iraq was already being prepared—was thrust for the first time into the center of the movement's political agenda. It was there that the call for worldwide antiwar rallies on February 15, 2003, was made. The process created strong ties. The second ESF was planned for November 2003 in Paris.

The Thematic Social Forum about peaceful solutions to conflicts, which brought together six hundred participants in Ramallah, Palestine, December 26–29, 2002, was an event filled with important symbolism, but which confronted huge political limitations. The Israeli government prohibited many European and U.S. participants from attending; those from Arab countries were summarily vetoed; the involvement of Israeli civil society organizations was limited; and those from Palestinian civil society confronted a series of difficulties, from Islamic fundamentalist groups on one hand to the Palestinian National Authority on the other. But it was an important opportunity for the region's progressive movements to interact with international solidarity movements.

A second African Social Forum (ASF) also met, focusing on the same issues within the framework of the first ASF, January 5–9, 2003, in Addis Ababa, Ethiopia.

The Asian Social Forum, which met in Hyderabad, in the Indian state of Andhra Pradesh, January 2–7, 2003, was another remarkable moment in the process of internationalization. More than 20,000 people participated, with 14,426 delegates and 800 young people in a beautiful Youth Camp. The Nizam College of Hyderabad was the location of eight large conferences, prepared in a centralized manner and held in two large tents capable of holding 3,000 people and in classrooms for 160 seminars and 164 workshops. The same festive spirit as the first WSF of Porto Alegre pervaded the event, with the additional element of the unbreakable link that the Indian Left had made between culture and politics. In a multicultural society, cultural activities are understood as a key part of political action, and they encompassed a large part of the Asian Social Forum program.

India is important not only because of its size and population, but also because of its political, ethnic, cultural, and religious complexity. However, the forum was also able to involve many organizations from neighboring countries, such as Nepal, Bangladesh, and even Pakistan—despite the difficulties imposed by the right-wing Indian government (the forum was held at the apex of the conflict between the two countries, trading rounds of gunfire in the province of Kashmir). In total, 840 delegates from outside India appeared at the Asian Social Forum.

The Asian Social Forum enabled a large number of movements and Asian organizations, and more importantly Indians, to integrate into the WSF process and to bring together the Left in that country. Finally, the country's adverse political reality, with an extremely right-wing central government that stirred up Hindu religious fundamentalism in a population with vast religious minorities and promoted all types of xenophobic affirmation of communal identities (which the Indians call "communalism"), had already pushed the fragmented Indian Left to take a more united stance. The WSF's legitimacy and its method of organizing facilitated this at the Asian Social Forum. This was, however, very characteristic of the Indian Left. With the inheritance of Gandhian socialism (party and nonparty); the impact of Maoism on the Indian communist movement in the 1960s (called "Naxalism"), and the multiplicity of parties calling themselves Marxist-Leninist, the challenges of renewal, respect for diversity, and collaborative relations are ever-present issues.

The success of the Asian Social Forum significantly expanded the WSF process beyond the Latin American—Western European axis. It demonstrated that conditions existed in India to hold the fourth WSF as a world event of an importance equivalent to Porto Alegre. This would bring to the WSF process in its assemblage important elements of renewal and enrichment of the agenda, discourses, and practices, as well as provide potential for the expansion of the global movement in Asia.

Even before the third WSF occurred, the second Pan-Amazon Social Forum was held in Belém, Brazil, January 16–19, 2003 (the first took place January 25–27, 2002). Its seven thousand participants debated a broad array of decisive questions for the region's movements and groups, including the environmental situation, the growing North American military presence in the Amazon, Plan Colombia, and fighting the FTAA.

All the richness created by the accelerated internationalization of the World Social Forum *process* was expressed in the meeting of the IC on January 21–22, 2003, in Porto Alegre. The IC was faced with a more pluralistic WSF, which incorporated new actors and was permeated with new tensions. It was the biggest and most combative IC meeting to date. The decisions adopted there addressed various contradictions that marked the WSF process and significantly altered its architecture, making the IC more representative of the worldwide movement.

The most important (and difficult) decision was to set the location of the fourth WSF in India in January 2004, and no longer in Porto Alegre, definitively consolidating its internationalization. For many, the logic "if it isn't broken, don't fix it" should have prevailed regarding a change in the location of the WSF. The meeting also approved that the WSF 2005 would again be held in Porto Alegre. This debate involved still other elements, such as the position that an intensification of the process should result in the organizing of a single World Social Forum every two years (not annually), in order to concentrate more energy on the regional forums. This debate continues.

Other far-reaching decisions were made: there would be no hierarchical relationship between the events in the process, meaning that individual social forums would not be seen as preparatory for larger regional forums or the WSF; the date of the WSF would be determined independently of the date of the Davos forum since the WSF is no longer only anti-Davos; and the forum would organize "Another World Is Possible: A Day of Protest against Neoliberalism and War" on some of the dates of the Davos meeting in 2004.

In addition to this, the experience gained and the increasing size of the mega-event and the problems presented by the organization of the third WSF already suggested the need for critical reflection on the forum's organizational issues: organizers could not spend as much energy on producing events, on one hand; on the other, activities autonomously organized by their proponents should have, in the different forums, at least as much weight as the ones proposed by forum organizers (reinforcing its character as an open and autonomously organized space).

A solution to the basic problem of the "power" of the process was established. This had been debated since Barcelona and focused on the composition of the International Council. As resolved, the IC would be open to the movements and organizations that accepted the WSF Charter of Principles and asked to join the WSF process. The Organizing Committee of the fourth WSF would be composed of Indian organizations. The WSF Secretariat would be composed of the eight Brazilian organizations that made up the old Brazilian Organizing Committee, and it would continue to act as a process facilitator. This Secretariat should be progressively internationalized.

The IC reinforced the definition of the WSF as a "horizontal space," and not a pyramidal organization, once again rejecting proposals that the IC issue declarations, which could be seen as directing the global movement. The success of the February 15 mobilizations against the war between the United States and the UK and Iraq, which brought tens of millions of people to the streets worldwide, demonstrated that relevant political initiatives can be coordinated and publicized by the forum without establishing a traditional directive process.

BOUND FOR INDIA

Starting with the parameters adopted in January 2003 in Porto Alegre, the success of the fourth WSF in India became the central challenge for the next step of the forum process. Holding the WSF in India would definitively assure the forum's internationalization.

Organizing the WSF in India required a complex structure, conceived to incorporate the largest number of organizations possible while still being able to accomplish the task. An Indian General Council, composed of around 150 organizations; an Indian Work Committee, with around 65 organizations involved in working groups; and an Indian Organizing Committee, with around 40 organizations and the central organizing body of the process, met monthly.

It was determined in March 2003 that the WSF would take place in Mumbai (formerly Bombay), January 16–21, 2004. This decision took into account the city's infrastructure, its accessibility to Indians and foreigners, its character as the most cosmopolitan city in the country, and the political equilibrium between the various sectors involved in the process. From there, the Mumbai Organizing Committee was formed. The base of preparatory work was done horizontally in open working groups: program, mobilization, youth, culture, local and logistical, finance, media and communication, and links. The proposal on how to format the event, formulated by the Indian Organizing Committee, had already been approved by the International Council.

The mobilization for the forum in Mumbai was initiated, particularly in Asia, by an important meeting of the support network on the continent, with participation by members of 120 organizations and movements, on June 1–2, 2003.

The internationalization of the WSF is not only focused on holding the forum in India. Initiatives have multiplied, as much on a local and national scale (with social forums for cities, regions, and countries, in an expansion impossible to keep up with) as on an international scale. Between June 16 and June 20, 2003, the Thematic Social Forum about democracy, human rights, war, and narcotrafficking was held in Cartageña, Colombia.

The only meeting of the International Council between the third and fourth World Social Forums was held in the United States, in Miami, Florida, June 23–26, 2003, taking advantage of the large number of groups that had been meeting earlier in that city for the tenth Jobs with Justice convention. The meeting was held in such a politically inhospitable place in order to increase the involvement of U.S. movements in the WSF process. This was important because of the perception of the strategic role and necessity for wider connections between groups and organizations inside and outside the empire in the fight against neoliberalism and war.

The main result of this meeting was to establish a commitment between the different sectors of the movement in the United States to identify with the WSF process, with a view to a common mobilization agenda for the years 2003 and 2004 and to hold the U.S. Social Forum in 2005. For 2004, the possibility was also raised of holding a thematic forum about globalization, militarization, and social struggles on the occasion of the Republican Party National Convention in New York at the end of August.*

A delegation of the Indian Organizing Committee, presenting its proposal for organizing the fourth WSF in January 2004 in Mumbai, also attended the Miami meeting. Questions about logistics and the WSF's functioning were received

---

*The Boston Social Forum took place in July 2004, on the eve of the Democratic National Convention in that city. More than 5,000 people participated. More than 500,000 marched in New York against the Bush agenda on the eve of the Republican National Convention.

positively, and the proposals regarding themes and methodology that had been presented in the IC were approved.

The Indian Organizing Committee foresaw holding on each one of the four full days of the forum (January 17–20), with the exception of the opening and closing, three panels in the morning, two hundred autonomously organized activities in the afternoon, as well as the testimonies and voices of resistance and a conference. The expectation of public attendance was seventy-five thousand participants. The organization of a Youth Camp for fifteen thousand participants was also anticipated.

For the WSF 2004, five themes focused on the struggle were proposed: against globalization and imperialism; patriarchy; militarization; sectarianism and fundamentalism; and caste discrimination and racism. The IC proposed that activities should be organized around four wide axes: militarism, war, and peace; information, knowledge, and culture; environment and economy; and exclusion, rights, and equality. The Miami meeting also reorganized the work of the IC into six commissions: strategy, methodology, content, communications, finance, and expansion. The functioning Secretariat in Brazil shared its experience of organizing the WSF with the Indian Committee.

Preparations for regional forums continued to advance as well. Before the fourth WSF, the second European Social Forum (ESF) was held November 12–15, 2003, in Paris. Preparatory meetings for the 2003 ESF took place in Saint-Denis, France; Brussels, Belgium; Berlin, Germany; and Thessalonia, Greece. At the Berlin meeting, a document that established a common understanding of the WSF process among all involved in its preparation was adopted. This document balanced distinct visions of the WSF process, which had previously polarized the French and Italian organizations. In a context in which the European unification on neoliberal grounds is intensifying and where the forum is a strict space for those who seek a progressive alternative to meet, discuss, and organize, everything indicated that the second ESF would repeat the political success of the first.

Various forums were planned to occur after Mumbai. The third Pan-Amazon Forum was held February 4–8, 2004, in Guayana City, Venezuela, following 2003 preparatory meetings in Boa Vista, Brazil, and in Caracas, Venezuela. The Social Forum of the Americas was held July 25–30, 2004, in Quito, Ecuador, following on organizational discussions held in Miami. The Mediterranean Social Forum was held in Barcelona, Spain, in March 2004, building on two preparatory assemblies held on May 3–4, 2003, in Casablanca, Morocco, and July 4–6 in Naples, Italy.

WSF: AN INITIAL BALANCE SHEET

The immense array of initiatives developed over almost three years of great political experimentation already allows us, with some degree of certainty, to make some key observations about the WSF.

The WSF is a *space* and not an *organization*. It creates a meeting place for dialogue, debate, and diffusion of proposals; exchanging experiences, emulating successes, developing battle plans, and organizing new movements. Despite demands for it to move in this direction, the forum is neither an embryo of an International nor a general staff of the movements that participate in it. The IC, Secretariat, and Organizing Committees of the forums work as facilitators of this political space: the forum does not issue positions as a body, and neither are there voting assemblies or final resolutions. Its vocation is, as such, to incorporate, in a pluralist form, increasingly large sectors that identify with the objectives of the struggle against neoliberalism, imperialism, and the war. Diversity is a strength and not a weakness of the WSF, and should be defended and supported. Any group or sector within the forum can meet and formulate whatever declaration, proposal, or position it wants (as the International Network of Social Movements has done since the first WSF). They do not, however, claim to speak on behalf of the forum or on behalf of those who have not explicitly signed on to their proposals. It is not within the mandate of the IC (or the Secretariat) to take positions, however correct they may be (against the war, for example), but to create the conditions for the movements and groups that participate in the forum to do what they will within the WSF framework. This is much more effective in the practical building of movements, as was demonstrated in the February 15, 2003, antiwar rallies.

The WSF is a *process* and not just an *event,* and it is *part of a bigger movement.* With the multiplication of forums, some organized at the continental level, others at the city level, the WSF has become a worldwide process. It helps to provide continuity to the new internationalism that, since Seattle, has been spreading around the world, confronting neoliberal globalization. The movement has come to be viewed as more than simply "antiglobalization," as it was initially characterized in the media. The multiplication of WSF spaces makes it possible for people to meet more frequently, establish ties and relationships of trust, and better coordinate their actions. It helps to create an environment that allows for the expansion of social movements and this new internationalism. However, even if the WSF is identified with all of the expressions of resistance and the searches for alternatives and wants to let them flourish in the spaces that it provides, it does not attempt to represent them, despite becoming an increasingly more central reference point for the "global movement."

The WSF is contributing to *altering the ideological climate* in today's world, helping to break the hegemony of the values of marketization, neoliberalism, and growing militarism. Giving voice to the fight against the commercialization of the world and affirming itself in opposition to multilateral organizations, the global movement as well as the WSF knows how to respond to the changes on the agenda that the Bush administration, with its unilateralism and its "war against terrorism," imposes on the international scene. Claiming spaces for values and libertarian political horizons has been happening in the forums, together with a collective education of how to confront the challenges that arise at each new step in the fight for another world.

This can happen because the WSF is organized in a manner that creates an autonomous learning experience for its participants. In the forum, all can present their concerns, organize their own activities, and participate in innumerable other activities, meeting with people from all places and sectors. If the colossal number of activities leaves a sense of fragmentation, a certain image of chaos, it also breaks through feelings of isolation, energizing its participants and exuding and transmitting confidence that the alternatives presented there express the belief of a significant part of society and of movements all over the planet that another world is possible. This *sense of living* is a remarkable characteristic of all the great events in the WSF process for its participants.

The forums also present themselves as a place of meeting in the strict sense, and of incorporating into the movement a *new political generation* that did not know the experiences, dramas, and defeats of the traditional left currents of the twentieth century. This generation is the backbone of the battles that will shape the Left of the twenty-first century, and the forums are the best space for developing new political initiatives and incubating new social movements.

Nevertheless, the WSF process has to deal with *important contradictions* in regard to its definition and scope. These structural contradictions can neither be suppressed nor overcome, at least not in the current organization of the forum (and probably for a certain period). These contradictions must be accepted and addressed as they come up, with participants developing what is positive and holding back potentially destructive elements. We live at a historic crossroads, a period of profound societal and political transformation, and the WSF not only gives voice to emerging forces but also holds within it many conceptions held over from the past.

The most evident contradiction is connected to the WSF's *relationship with political parties.* The Charter of Principles establishes that parties, governments, and armed organizations neither organize the WSF nor send delegates to the events. The forum opts, as such, to be a refuge for expressions by civil society that are today less permeated by political power disputes, but also less committed to defending the status quo. Exactly for this reason are the social movements more decisive for the strategic recomposition of the world Left. It is they—much more than the traditional political parties of the Left—that drive the resistance and fundamental struggles under way and spark the debate on the construction of alternatives. The forum can encourage debate on the crisis in political representation in the sectors active in the fight around the world. The alternative of allowing parties to join the WSF—given the current state of political party organization worldwide—would bring disastrous consequences to the forums. To do so probably would introduce tensions impossible to control, and would tend to repeat experiences such as that of the São Paulo Forum (established by leftist parties in Latin America in the beginning of the 1990s and currently a mere point of contact for diplomatic relations).

The forum is not free from contact with parties. All of the old and new political currents present in the organizations and movements end up expressing themselves in the WSF. The more attuned to the fights and the global movement they are, the more presence these currents have, through their militants, at the forums. The forums have organized parallel spaces and types of activities (such as the dialogue-and-controversy roundtables in the third WSF) in order to debate with parties, governments, parliamentarians, and multilateral institutions. However, the tensions exist and will remain permanent as long as the crisis in party representation continues.

On the other hand, the positive relationship between diverse political initiatives and the WSF process, acting according to the rules established in the Charter of Principles, is an indicator of its capacity today to sharpen and broaden the global movement. In this sense, we can say that one of the virtues of the forum is that it can, at this current stage in history, contribute to and, what's more, accelerate the political recomposition of the Left on different political terrains. Therefore, it can help to overcome the leftist parties' crisis of political representation. Obviously, to consciously work in this more indirect way is different from advocating that the political parties participate today as organizers of the forums.

The crisis of political representation of the Left and the indirect participation of the parties in the WSF bring about a *demand that the forum itself fulfill the role of leadership.* But the forums are spaces, and the IC, the Secretariat, and the Organizing Committees are facilitators of the functioning of these spaces. They are able only to present proposals for directing the WSF process and for preparing its events—indirectly influencing the direction of the movement without commanding it. The current movement and the forum, in other words, form a network, not a pyramid linked to a historical epoch (of Fordism, in the analogy of parties and the armies, etc.) that is passing. Nevertheless, these analogies evoke logics that to a great degree contradict each other.

In this context, the connection between the politics of the wider movement (of which the WSF is a part) and the diverse events on which the forum grounds itself is achieved by distinct organizations, movements, and networks that take on the challenge. If the WSF, the movement, and its political sensibilities are averse to a traditional idea of political leadership, this does not eliminate the need for the movement to determine its priorities. Since 2001, with the first WSF, what is now the International Network of Social Movements has been playing a certain role in the development of the movement and its battles. Its ability to function is doubly limited, however. On one hand, in the WSF, it cannot speak for the movement in all of its parts gathered at the forum. It must firmly defend the diversity and pluralism of the process and avoid the narrowing of its composition. On the other hand, in the wider movement, the International Network of Social Movements is constrained by the actions of political party organizations that compete for a leadership role in the movement.

Again, we have here a permanent tension that will have to be worked out within the WSF process. The forum bodies (IC, Secretariat, organizing committees) have to be legitimate facilitators, accepting competing and conflicting roles, patiently dealing with disputes, being open to new forces in the movement, and resisting the temptation to suppress differences or to assume a commanding leadership role.

What emerges from this framework is a vast, diversified, patient, and sometimes contradictory collective work of reconstructing the historically weak world Left's ability to shape events, while its destiny is linked to the battles of the multifaceted global movement. The future of the WSF will be, therefore, affected profoundly by the shocks of the reconfiguration of the Left and of the world political landscape stemming from the Bush doctrine of preventive war, the emergence of new interimperialistic conflicts within multilateral institutions, and the agreements on the management (and repartition) of the global market (within the WTO, FTAA, and the European Union). The gigantic antiwar movement, which increasingly took on the appearance of a movement against the North American empire, points to the potential of the global movement and of the WSF process in the near term. However, a welding together of the fight against neoliberalism and the fight against the war must continue as developments unfold.

What is certain is that new challenges will emerge at each moment of the World Social Forum process. The form that that they will take will determine whether the forum will continue to catalyze the energies of a good part of the global movement, and whether it is a central political space for the Left in the twenty-first century.

EPILOGUE

New Directions for the World Social Forum

The fourth World Social Forum (WSF), held in Mumbai, India, on January 16–21, 2004, proved the vitality of the WSF format and the "open space" method that has been built gradually in the three Porto Alegre forums, the two European Social Forums (Florence and Paris), and the Asian Social Forum (Hyderabad), as well as countless other forums. The Mumbai forum renewed and expanded the reach of the proposal, generating a wave of energy in the process. However, after three years, there is a general perception that the forum needs to change directions, focusing especially on the development of actions capable of influencing the balance of world power. This was the focus in the International Council (IC), which gathered in Mumbai before, during, and after the WSF to discuss preparations for the fifth WSF, to be held in Porto Alegre, Brazil, in January 2005.

WSF 2004 was a remarkable global event: 74,126 registered delegates (60,224 from India and 13,902 foreigners) from 117 countries representing 1,635 organizations (838 Indian and 797 from abroad). In addition, forty thousand passes were issued to people who took part in the activities for one day only or to those who could not afford the registration fee. The presence of another four thousand participants in the Youth Camp, volunteers who worked for the event, and the people from Mumbai who attended the open activities must be included as well. An estimated 135,000–150,000 people took part in the 1,200 WSF activities.

WSF 2004 had a great impact on the Indian Left. India is marked by regionalism, communalism, and diversity in languages, religions, and cultures. The forum had been planned since 2002; in fact, the Asian Social Forum in January 2003 was its "rehearsal." It was held in a more pluralistic and demanding context than previous WSFs, owing to the greater heterogeneity in the Indian Left. WSF 2004 required the united action of organizations from disparate political traditions—from Gandhian nonviolence to the more traditional communist parties, from various Maoist organizations to NGOs. This unity was carefully built thanks to a broad process of preparation and mobilization in the different regions in the country. This is why the forum was marked—within its Charter of Principles—by a less reticent posture toward political parties, erasing the sense that they are outside of or foreign to the forum or to the struggle to which the WSF is connected.

The Mumbai forum definitely connected the struggle against neoliberalism with the struggle against militarization and empire. To the delegates present in Mumbai, the struggle against poverty and exclusion resulting from capitalist globalization was inseparable from the struggle against war and imperialism. This forum also included issues previously ignored or put aside on the global movement's agenda, such as the struggle against caste discrimination, which keeps 200 million Indians on the periphery of society and requires a rethinking of the problem of racism and the struggle against the combined effects of communalism, sexism, and religious fundamentalism—all of which had received boosts from the fundamentalist Hindu government in New Delhi and the more conservative social climate following the September 11 attacks.

Therefore, the fourth WSF took place in a context far removed from Western political culture. The event was highly popular, militant, and feminist—reinforced by the massive presence of popular movements not only from India, but also from most parts of Asia. In Asia, the forum has become a space for activities that are, first and foremost, protests and invitations to political action. Mumbai and the Indian Organizing Committee (IOC) have qualitatively enriched the WSF process, introducing several elements that must be considered in future initiatives.

THE MUMBAI EFFECT

The IOC, formed by forty-eight different organizations, took a long time to choose the city to host the fourth WSF. But its final decision on Mumbai turned out to be more than justified. Mumbai, formerly called Bombay, has a weak Left presence and is ruled by the extreme Right—what an impact on forum participants those two facts had! Even for those who have been to India before, staying a week in the neighborhood of the exhibition park NESCO Grounds, in Goregaon, in the northern edge of Greater Mumbai (30 km from Colaba, south of the peninsula, the financial and tourist "city center") was a living lesson in the results of globalization as suffered by billions of people.

Mumbai is the biggest city in India. It has 16.4 million inhabitants according to the latest census and competes with São Paulo for the position of the third most populous city on Earth. Mumbai inhabitants are crushed into an area that is less than 10 percent the size of Greater São Paulo. (The city of Mumbai is only 440 square kilometers in size, while the city of São Paulo is 1,509 square kilometers.) One million people survive on Mumbai's streets. Some of Mumbai's avenues are half taken over by huts.

The rural population, which represented 75 percent of the 1.03 billion Indians registered in 2001, stream to Mumbai in large numbers. The environment is totally ruined. Dust and pollution fill the air just a few hundred meters away from the sea. If one does not take a full train, chaotic traffic makes the journey from the city's center to its edge last two hours. At the same time, Mumbai is the only global metropolis in India. Mila Kahlon writes:

> In this sense, this city is the only truly metropolitan one in India. Compared to it, Chennai (Madras), Calcutta, Bangalore (the silicon valley of India) or even the capital New Delhi seem narrow-minded provincial towns. This may be hard for an outsider to understand, but India's rural population is stuck in the 18th century, so in this context my city is a miracle, a true dream city, and without doubt the wealthiest in India. More than half of India's income tax is paid here.
>
> It is also India's most corrupt city: more than half of the black money in circulation is generated here. It has more millionaires than the other metropolitan cities put together. It hosts 90% of India's merchant banking transactions and has

two stock exchange towers; 80% of India's mutual funds are registered here, where the capital markets are located. India's central bank, three largest retail banks and two largest commercial lenders are based in the business district.

Its ports handle 40% of India's maritime trade. Real estate means money—property is more expensive than in New York and Tokyo (a posh apartment could cost up to $2m). This city indulges in speculations, lotteries, horse races and cricket. Advertising hotshots are better paid than doctors, as Mumbaikars shame the consumer society of the United States. The city attracts the best skill pool in India, multinational giants, investors, artists and intellectuals.

The glitter of Bollywood is irresistible: the city has the biggest film industry in the world and any Indian cinema wannabe comes here, youngsters from all backgrounds and classes want to be part of it; retired and forgotten stars from the West sign contracts for guest appearances in Hindi movies with the hope of a second lease of life. Actors are viewed as gods and behave like gods. The film crowd lives in mansions in swanky suburbs in fear of mafia dons who derive their income from extortion money.*

Mumbai is a microcosm of India, surely the most diverse society in the world. Its population spans every color and speaks eighteen official languages and sixteen hundred languages and dialects. The forum had to adopt English as the language used in the main events (with translation into five other Indian languages and foreign languages) because the Indo-European languages (Hindi, spoken by only 20 percent of Indians; Marathi, dominant in the Mumbai region; and Bengali) are not understood by those who speak Dravidian languages, and vice versa.

---

*Mila Kahlon, "India's City of Gold," *Le Monde Diplomatique,* January 2004.

India is mostly Hindu (82 percent), but it also includes an Islamic minority (12 percent), nineteen million Christians, eighteen million Sikhs, seven million Buddhists, four million Jains, and many expressing other beliefs. Communalist conflicts have increased (especially due to the persecution of Muslims), spurred by the nationalist Hindu currents, which from 1998 to 2004 controlled the central government and kept a militarist and nuclear policy toward Pakistan and China. One such party, Shiv Sena (Shivaji Army), has ruled Mumbai since 1985 and shared the government of Maharashtra since 1995 with the reactionary Bharatiya Janata Party (BJP), which led the central government until it was voted out of office in May 2004. It was Baja's government in Gujarat State that allowed two thousand Muslims to be killed by fanatic Hindus in March 2002.

In the last decade, the successive coalitions in power in India have applied a neoliberal policy, which has increased economic growth but has also contributed to the economy's financialization and its susceptibility to external shocks. This policy has greatly widened the gap between rich and poor and eliminated social welfare policies, increasing exclusion in different ways.

The organizers of the fourth WSF made real to participants the shock of unequal development—with fantastic postmodern towers raised in huge slums, with cosmopolitan global elites living alongside a miserable rural India stuck in the eighteenth century. Billionaires and the affluent middle class live without apology in midst of countless Dalits, people who fight every single day for survival. This experience provided, even for Latin American participants, an existential redefinition of the misery and exclusion caused by neoliberal globalization.

ESTABLISHMENT AND ENRICHMENT OF THE PROCESS

The most visible conflicts in Indian society derive from the complex system of castes associated with Hinduism. Put very plainly, it is believed that if an individual follows the duties of his caste, his chances of rebirth in a superior caste and in better circumstances increase. This situation is particularly unsustainable for more than 200 million Dalits (formerly known as "untouchables") who make up the lowest caste. They are discriminated against in every aspect of society and are spread across dozens of different movements.

Patriarchy strongly influences the situation of women, who are oppressed by practices ranging from dowry to abortion of female fetuses, from widow burning* to women's double burden of working both inside and outside the home. In a society where families arrange the majority of marriages, winning autonomy is still a difficult proposition for most women.

In addition to these oppressions, there is the situation of the Adivasis, tribal communities that include between fifty-five million and sixty million people who have been expropriated from their ancestral lands and impoverished after a thousand years of contact with the Hindu and Muslim populations.

These sectors most notably brought their problems and struggles to the fourth WSF—especially the Dalits, who made up nearly half of the Indian delegates. The most urgent

---

* The Hindu rite of *sati* required a widow to throw herself on her husband's funeral pyre. The British banned the practice in the nineteenth century. Today, devout widows are supposed to shave their heads, remove all personal adornments, and never marry again after their husbands die.

problems in these people's lives, which their delegates understood to be linked to neoliberal globalization, motivated the majority of discussions that occurred in Nesco Grounds. In addition to the class issues established by the communist or socialist Left, another great range of inquiries, emerging more directly from the fight against caste oppression, communalism, religious sectarianism, and patriarchalism, earned centrality in the forum.

The renewal of the WSF process in Mumbai was amplified by the strong presence of the Asian delegations—from Pakistan to Japan, from Bangladesh to the Philippines, from Palestine to Afghanistan. Exiled Tibetan monks marched side by side with participants of popular movements in Thailand; activists against war in Central Asian countries and in the Muslim world stood with Korean trade-union militants. Their problems, cultures, organizational forms, and political practices raised many questions that will take time for the WSF process to assimilate.

For a large number of the delegates present in Mumbai, the international political agenda had a clear focus: the fight against the Bush government, North American imperialism, and its military offensive. This was the core of the discussions about Iraq, Afghanistan, Korea, and Palestine, to name the areas that were most featured. Of course the fight against the free-trade agreements that have multiplied in the region was discussed, as were the struggle against the expulsion of immigrant workers in Korea and Japan and the fights for arms control, for making Tibet a peace zone, and for food security and preservation of biodiversity and natural resources, etc. However, nothing surpassed the force of the fight against the threat to the world represented by Bush's government. That explains the wide support for the proposal by the General Assembly of the Global Movement Against War for a global day of action on March 20 against the occupation in Iraq—on the first anniversary of the U.S. invasion of that country.

In general, the fourth WSF seemed thematically less dispersed than the third, particularly if one considers, in addition to the conferences, roundtables, and talks, the thirty-one big panel meetings. The IOC capably managed to organize large events that also had strong political content.

The popular character of the fourth WSF stemmed largely from the broad way in which the event was organized. This included an Indian Organizing Committee that spanned almost every progressive movement in the country and an Asian support network that held two very representative meetings, in Chennai and Mumbai, before the WSF. All of this meant a strong effort to achieve dialogue and political understanding, expressed in the Mumbai event in a pluralism of perspectives and an evolution of the movements. The forum also was preceded by a large regional mobilization, essential for the success of a national event in India, with forums and demonstrations in several Indian states. As Pierre Rousset notes:

> This unifying dynamic has no precedent in India and created a convergence among environments and movements often far removed from each other. Since December 6, 2003, associations of dalit "untouchables" had been organising "dignity marches" converging on Mumbai; aboriginal tribes too were very active at the forum, brandishing their bows and arrows. This self-assertion by the lowest castes and the casteless ensured the presence of workers from the economy's informal sector, joining those from the formal sector where trade

unions are better established. Associations that refuse all international funding collaborated with NGOs that accept it. Gandhi-inspired "grassroots movements" met up again with traditional mass movements linked to left-wing parties.

A doubly unifying dynamic was thus set up during preparation of the WSF: at the national level, among movements that are very different in kind and, at the local level, with the multitude of regional associations. These were two (of the many) conditions for its success.*

To the WSF, Mumbai represented a giant qualitative step in the scope of the dialogue that the forum facilitates and in the social roots it establishes. From the point of view of "the struggle for another world," this was probably the most important step since the forum process began in January 2001. Only a successful follow-up will tell whether the forum will be able to bring together struggles in the West with those in other world regions, which cannot be subsumed under any common label.

ORGANIZATIONAL AND METHODOLOGICAL INITIATIVES

The decisive logistical decision in Mumbai was to concentrate the activities in one place rather than to disperse them. That helped to sustain the energetic and vital mood in the fourth WSF. The forum was carried out in an abandoned textile complex that now serves as an events center, which forum organizers creatively transformed so that it could house the multiple planned activities. We did not have, as in Porto Alegre, the classrooms and the PUC (university) infrastructure, but this did not hinder activities. The critical note

---

* Pierre Rousset, "World Social Forum at Mumbai: Reflecting on Conditions for Success," March 1, 2004, at www.forumsocialmundial.org.br.

is related to the Youth Camp, which was far smaller than the one in Porto Alegre. The camp was located in the area belonging to a Catholic high school ten kilometers away, making youth involvement in the forum more difficult.

The popular and militant character of the fourth WSF resulted in part from the efforts and resources dedicated to the cultural dimension of the event, conceived not as "entertainment" or a "show," but essentially as political expression. Since the Asian Social Forum, it was clear that Indians put a different emphasis on cultural issues, making a political approach to the cultural dimension more suitable than in the previous forums. The cultural initiatives were not shows by professional artists, but they were part of the current struggles in communities and movements. Even the exhibition of "Western" cinema was conceived by many cultural activists as embracing organic components of the forum.

A network of volunteers translated talks into local languages as well as Spanish, French, Korean, Japanese, Thai, Malay, and Indonesian (Bahasa). This international network, Babels, formed in the European Social Forum, today includes more than 4,500 interpreters and 1,500 translators. It represents a great advance in the area of translation, allowing different actors in the movement to express themselves in their own languages. In India, 180 translators worked with Babels.

This network introduced a new tool in Mumbai, through the French collective of sound artists Apo33: a computer program based in free software, called Nomad, that allows instant digitization of every speech (from the speaker and the translators, too). Therefore, each room equipped with the Nomad system has a computer network that performs different functions: voice transmission (digital or FM), storage and classification of the debates, coordination of translation, and Internet transmission of sound and video archives. In India, after problems on the first day that stemmed from improvised electrical installations, it passed the test. Nomad makes it increasingly possible for forum activities to be attended in "real time" by people all over the world, listening in their own languages if they are among those adopted for simultaneous translation. This tool opens tremendous possibilities to the internationalist movement.

From the methodological point of view, the Mumbai forum was different from previous forums in that the Indian Organizing Committee, with support from the IC, organized only a few activities. Among the forty-eight activities organized for more than four thousand people in WSF 2004, thirteen were the responsibility of the IOC and thirty-five were "self-organized" (proposed and organized by the participants themselves and chosen from among the more than two hundred submitted). Nevertheless, some of these large activities had low attendance. The most lively debates were, more than in Porto Alegre, principally found in medium-size events, which were able to attract sizable crowds, but were not so big as to stifle dialogue among those present.

Despite the effort of the IOC to enforce the registration deadline for activities and to promote the fusion of events (which reduced the number of activities from 2,000 to about 1,200), duplication of activities still occurred by organizations that had not shared workshops and seminars or even exceeded the limit of four events per participating organization. Amit Sen Gupta, from the Indian group handling programming and methodology, observed that "the cooperative culture is still developing in the WSF and the resistance to working together in specific activities still is a formidable obstacle among us."

POLITICAL PARTIES AND THE FORUM

Mumbai reaffirmed the understanding that the forum is an open political space established by the Charter of Principles of the WSF. Today almost everyone on the Left knows that the forum does not accept resolutions and that political parties and guerrilla organizations do not participate in the organizing of the WSF and the reasoning behind these policies. They also know that political parties are not unwelcome guests; in fact, they are important participants in the process, and the forum dialogues with them and wants to empower them. The ground rules, although strange to those from other political cultures, are questioned less and less.

In Mumbai, a clear political delimitation originated. We had parallel events organized to coincide with the forum—which the IOC wisely treated as complementary initiatives. The most important one was the Mumbai Resistance 2004, organized by a small international network of Maoist parties through their mass fronts. They had questioned the idea of open space, the fact that the forum does not take resolutions, its lack of an explicitly socialist character, and the fact that it does not endorse armed struggle in movements for social change. Also, there was the People's Encounter II, whose promoters had broken with the WSF process because they did not accept working with mass organizations that identified themselves with political parties. Participants in these events, as well as some participants in the forum itself, warned that the international financial ties of certain organizations in the forum served to influence and moderate the forum's political agenda. In the end, the parallel events had marginal participation, showing that the WSF process was able to offer a broad and united discussion.

In fact, the relationship between social movements and political parties took an important step, however, with the fourth WSF. Until then, the Brazilian reality—where most of the participants had supported the PT, which meant that the best option had been to keep the PT as an institution outside the process—had informed, in large part, the relationship between political parties and the forum. The political culture dominant in some European countries, such as Italy and England, had brought to the process some questions about the form posed by the Charter of Principles (which naturally conditions its results). These questions were resolved in the European Social Forum.

The Mumbai experience introduced new elements. Very heterogeneous from the political point of view, the Indian Left had found in the forum's formula a practical method of building urgently needed unity. Pressured by Hindu fundamentalism and religious sectarianism and struggling with an extreme-right government that threatened the gains made since independence, the Indian Left had shown that today almost every single political formation—from parties born in the official Communist movement to Gandhian socialism—can deal positively with the method of open space.

The great Left traditions in the world are reacting to the reality established by the WSF process. In 2003, a gathering of social-democratic currents in Belgium determined that they should seek a more active role in the process. In Mumbai, communist parties participated in the forum, merging the issue of how to deal with their pasts—particularly the Soviet experience and Stalinism—with the present and future.

However, most revealing of the coming together of the global movement and the WSF on the reorganization of the global Left was the meeting on January 20 in Mumbai among "radical" political parties, called at the initiative of the European meeting of anticapitalist parties and the Asia-Pacific political currents. For the first time, distinct currents—from Trotskyism to Maoism, from the official communist parties to the critics of Marxism—met, debated the new situation of the Left in the world, and created a network to continue this dialogue.

Several of these parties have met in the fourth World Parliamentarians Forum (WPF), which had formed as the parallel event for parliament members who identified with the proposals debated in the forum. The WPF has a different structure from the WSF—for example, voting on a final declaration, sometimes after a great deal of controversy (such as the position on the U.S. attack in Afghanistan, which polarized the second WPF). This time, the debate was less acrimonious. From this body of initiatives, it seems clear that slowly a very positive modus vivendi is developing between political parties and the forum process (and vice versa).

NEED TO CHANGE DIRECTION

Mumbai enriched the WSF agenda and integrated new and important forces in the process. It also increased the desire among forum participants to make the WSF a new and more useful tool to increase political action and to change the current relationships between political forces. The more neoliberalism seems a spent force, the more this aspiration is nourished. At last, the forum is not an end in itself but a means to allow thousands of movements in the world to articulate and strengthen their struggles. In Mumbai, with the successful staging of the forum in one the most conflicted and populous zones on the planet, this desire has gained a sense of urgency. Several critical discussions and self-criticisms among process proponents have expressed the need to change direction in the lead-up to Porto Alegre 2005.

What assessment can be made today about the forum's role in proposing our alternatives? One aspect seems clear: the forum process has created meeting places for the forces in the world that oppose the system. Many events and protests originating in the social forum movement have given shape and motivation to a common agenda of international mobilization. The protests against the war on Iraq on February 15, 2003, as well as demonstrations against the WTO meeting in Cancún on September 13, 2003, were the focus of debates in the WSF process in 2002 and 2003. A clear call for demonstrations on March 20, 2004—the first anniversary of the U.S. invasion of Iraq—came up in Mumbai as well. Establishing a common agenda for movements with the capacity for militant activity has been, in fact, the practical role of the assemblies in the World Network of Social Movements, and now also the General Assembly of the Global Movement against War.

Has the WSF process empowered the struggles and national mobilizations? On this question, the balance sheet is much less clear. The role of the forum is more indirect and uneven. An interesting dynamic seems to have been established in the relationship between regional and national organizing in

Western Europe, through the European Social Forum, although it is too early to provide a definitive evaluation. In the near future, we can also study the strategic results of the process in India. However, after three years it seems clear that we have a problem in rooting the forum in everyday struggles in the cases of Brazil and Latin America—although the continental campaign against the FTAA has been empowered by the forum process. The fifth WSF must complete its mission of creating a new political culture in the country and region.

MAKING THE FORUM MORE USEFUL TO THE MOVEMENTS

Changes at the national level are still limited, raising questions about whether the WSF is rooted in the mass movements in each community and nation. This seems to be the basis of the proposal by Via Campesina and other entities that the forum should occur every two years in order to channel more energy to local forums, which should alternate with global ones. Not denying the usefulness of the WSF as a space for making proposals but underlining the experience and educational benefits to participants, they propose moving to another phase in the process. This was also the basis of discussions at the IC meeting in Mumbai and of the decision to structure Porto Alegre 2005 to encourage discussions of strategy and proposals for action.

Articulation and formulation of plans of action should be put in the proper context, however. When one demands that the forum make alternatives, proposals, and plans of action viable, in fact, one is demanding a change in the correlation of social forces, which can come only from a *process of cross-pol-*

lination between the forum and thousands of movements and national and local entities. Some actions, such as the proposal by Arundhati Roy in the opening at Mumbai to boycott systematically two big and emblematic corporations of neoliberal globalization, can be made viable in forums such as the present ones. That is not the same for dozens of proposals that are already becoming closely associated with the global movement. In order to make such a change to the correlation of forces, we would need to make a great qualitative jump politically and organizationally, enabling the concentration and championing at the international level of a great number of national struggles and mobilizations.

The fact is that the forum is still much more a sequence of events than a permanent process. As an event, it ought to have a festive, media-friendly aspect, in order to increase its impact. Some critics still inveigh against this essentially positive dimension of the process (how is it different from transforming the forum into a show?), but the behind-the-scenes problem is another one, that of the *structural relationship between the forum and the wider movement* that gives it meaning.

Important steps were taken in Mumbai in defining a new shape for the event, based on self-organized activities. However, moving the forum process forward is not only a question of setting registration dates and matching up similar proposals; *it presupposes also condensing the network of relationships among thousands of entities and movements* all over the world. That makes the event a meeting place in the ongoing organization of vast networks of actors. There are already many thematic networks and very important campaigns. When the Brazilian Organizing Committee followed, in the second and third WSF, the movements' pressure for participation in the featured events, it had reached more than thirty thematic nuclei. *How to bring these thematic or sectoral foci inside the forum in open dialogue while maintaining their own dynamics* is, as already asserted by the female Indian comrades, a great organizational and political challenge for the WSF. It demands a huge investment of time, morale, and communication. Bringing into the WSF process hundreds of dispersed initiatives raises another challenge. A network structure works only if it pulls together efficient and well-positioned parts of the whole. *The WSF architecture must evolve with the process.* The initial structure of organizing committees and the International Council proved insufficient when the forum internationalized itself. The WSF Secretariat was introduced, today shared between the Brazilian and Indian Organizing Committees, and the International Council structured itself into working committees.

The challenges today are transitory. The IC, which was created between the first and second WSFs, froze its composition immediately after the second WSF. It had great difficulty in dealing with the expansion of the process and its becoming more pluralistic. This became unsustainable when organization spread to Asia, which does not have entities similar in structure to the IC (especially the international networks of NGOs and large trade-union confederations with access to international travel). In addition, mentalities and postures characteristic of hierarchical international organizations still conflict fundamentally with network conceptions and practices. Finally, the limitations of the regional processes still did not make viable the constitution of a sufficient number of nuclei to facilitate the process, in order to naturally redefine the functions between a qualitatively wider and more pluralistic IC, with a more political and less organizational role, and these nuclei, with the ability to act collectively and on day-to-day matters. The process architecture will be shaped and assisted, in large part, by the development of the regional forums, the experiences provided by them, and the constitution of organizational collectives that are socially rooted and emerge as organizing committees.

The consolidation of regional forums still must overcome several obstacles. It is not enough that a group of entities from a certain area has the willingness or even the material resources for making a regional forum process viable and stable. The real processes flow through central countries in each region, in which the structure of civil society is more solid and the political situation more secure. The search of alternative ways of organizing may here be a disaster. Besides, the regions (almost) never are continents in the geographic sense—for example, if there is a more stable identity of Europe (Western) or even America (Latin), there are many Asias, far beyond the Indian subcontinent, regions that must find their own paths. We must strike a delicate balance between trying to avoid substituting the wishes of the IC for local initiatives and effectively supporting the most fruitful initiatives.

Thus, the format of WSF 2005—as a friendly and efficient process in the development of proposals and political action to accomplish them—can lead to a qualitative jump in consolidating the WSF process only if it links concretely to international campaigns and networks. Moreover, this process will have to be rooted in a certain number of stable regional forums that function according to their own local dynamics. The challenges are not small, but they are surmountable.

NAOMI KLEIN

A Fête for the End of the End of History

"We are here to show the world that another world is possible!" the man on stage said, and a crowd of more than 10,000 roared its approval. What was strange was that we weren't cheering for a specific other world, just the possibility of one. We were cheering for the idea that another world could, in theory, exist.

For the past thirty years, a select group of CEOs and world leaders have met during the last week in January on a mountaintop in Switzerland to do what they presumed they were the only ones capable of doing: determine how the global economy should be governed. We were cheering because it was, in fact, the last week of January, and this wasn't the World Economic Forum in Davos, Switzerland. It was the first annual World Social Forum in Porto Alegre, Brazil. And even though we weren't CEOs or world leaders, we were still going to spend the week talking about how the global economy should be governed.

Originally published in the *Nation,* March 19, 2001. Reprinted with permission of the author.

Many people said that they felt history being made in that room. What I felt was something more intangible: the end of The End of History. And fittingly, "Another World Is Possible" was the event's official slogan. After a year and a half of protests against the World Trade Organization, the World Bank and the International Monetary Fund, the World Social Forum was billed as an opportunity for this emerging movement to stop screaming about what it is against and start articulating what it is for.

If Seattle was, for many people, the coming-out party of a resistance movement, then, according to Soren Ambrose, policy analyst with 50 Years Is Enough, "Porto Alegre is the coming-out party for the existence of serious thinking about alternatives." The emphasis was on alternatives coming from the countries experiencing most acutely the negative effects of globalization: mass migration of people, widening wealth disparities, weakening political power.

The particular site was chosen because Brazil's Workers Party (Partido dos Trabalhadores, the PT) is in power in the city of Porto Alegre, as well as in the state of Rio Grande do Sul. The conference was organized by a network of Brazilian unions and NGOs, but the PT provided state-of-the-art conference facilities at the Catholic University of Porto Alegre and paid the bill for a star-studded roster of speakers. Having a progressive government sponsor was a departure for a group of people accustomed to being met with clouds of pepper spray, border strip searches and no-protest zones. In Porto Alegre, activists were welcomed by friendly police officers and greeters with official banners from the tourism department.

Though the conference was locally organized, it was, in

part, the brainchild of ATTAC France, a coalition of unions, farmers and intellectuals that has become the most public face of the antiglobalization movement in much of Europe and Scandinavia. (ATTAC stands for Association for the Taxation of Financial Transactions for the Aid of Citizens, which, admittedly, doesn't work as well in English.) Founded in 1998 by Bernard Cassen and Susan George of the socialist monthly *Le Monde Diplomatique,* ATTAC began as a campaign for the implementation of the so-called Tobin Tax, the proposal by Nobel laureate James Tobin to tax all speculative financial transactions. Reflecting its Marxist intellectual roots, the group has expressed frustration with the less coherent focus of the North American anticorporate movement. "The failure of Seattle was the inability to come up with a common agenda, a global alliance at the world level to fight against globalization," says Christophe Aguiton of ATTAC, who helped organize the forum.

Which is where the World Social Forum came in: ATTAC saw the conference as an opportunity to bring together the best minds working on alternatives to neoliberal economic policies—not just new systems of taxation but everything from sustainable farming to participatory democracy to cooperative production to independent media. From this process of information swapping ATTAC believed its "common agenda" would emerge.

The result of the gathering was something much more complicated—as much chaos as cohesion, as much division as unity. In Porto Alegre the coalition of forces that often goes under the banner of antiglobalization began collectively to recast itself as a pro-democracy movement. In the process, the movement was also forced to confront the weaknesses of its own internal democracy and to ask difficult questions about how decisions were being made—at the World Social Forum itself and, more important, in the high-stakes planning for the next round of World Trade Organization negotiations and the Summit of the Americas in Quebec City at the end of April.

Part of the challenge was that the organizers had no idea how many people would be drawn to this Davos for activists. Atila Roque, a coordinator of IBASE, a Brazilian policy institute and a member of the organizing committee, explains that for months they thought they were planning a gathering of 2,000 people. Then, suddenly, there were 10,000, more at some events, representing 1,000 groups, from 120 countries. Most of those delegates had no idea what they were getting into: a model UN? A giant teach-in? An activist political convention? A party?

The result was a strange hybrid of all of the above, along with—at the opening ceremony at least—a little bit of Vegas floor show mixed in. On the first day of the forum, after the speeches finished and we cheered fanatically for the end of The End of History, the house lights went down and two giant screens projected photographs of poverty in Rio's *favelas*. A line of dancers appeared on stage, heads bowed in shame, feet shuffling. Slowly, the photographs became more hopeful, and the people on stage began to run, brandishing the tools of their empowerment: hammers, saws, bricks, axes, books, pens, computer keyboards, raised fists. In the final scene, a pregnant woman planted seeds—seeds, we were told, of another world.

What was jarring was not so much that this particular genre of utopian socialist dance had rarely been staged since the

WPA performances of the 1930s, but that it was done with such top-notch production values: perfect acoustics, professional lighting, headsets simultaneously translating the narration into four languages. All 10,000 of us were given little bags of seeds to take and plant at home. This was Soviet Realism meets *Cats*.

The forum was filled with these strange juxtapositions between underground ideas and Brazil's enthusiastic celebrity culture: mustachioed local politicians accompanied by glamorous wives in backless white dresses rubbing shoulders with the president of the Landless Peasants Movement of Brazil, known for chopping down fences and occupying large pieces of unused farmland. An old woman from Argentina's Mothers of the Plaza de Mayo, with her missing child's name crocheted on her white head scarf, quietly sitting next to a Brazilian soccer star so adored that his presence provoked several hardened politicos to rip off pieces of their clothing and demand autographs. José Bové, the French cheese farmer known for "strategically dismantling" a McDonald's, unable to go anywhere without a line of bodyguards protecting him from the *paparazzi*.

Every night the conference adjourned to an outdoor amphitheater where musicians from around the world performed, including the Cuarteto Patria, one of the Cuban bands made famous by Wim Wenders's documentary *The Buena Vista Social Club*. Cuban anything was big here. Speakers had only to mention the existence of the island nation for the room to break out in chants of *Cuba! Cuba! Cuba!* Chanting, it must be said, was also big: Not just for Cuba but for former presidential candidate and honorary president of the Workers Party Luiz Inácio Lula da Silva ("Lula-la"). José

Bové, after almost landing in jail for teaming up with local landless activists and destroying several hectares of genetically engineered soy beans, earned his very own chant: *Olé, Olé, Bové, Bové,* sung as a soccer stadium hymn.

One thing that wasn't so big at the World Social Forum was the United States. There were daily protests against Plan Colombia, the "wall of death" between the United States and Mexico, as well as George W. Bush's announcement that the new administration will suspend foreign aid to groups that provide information on abortion. In the workshops and lectures there was much talk of American imperialism, of the tyranny of the English language. Actual US citizens, though, were notably scarce. The AFL-CIO barely had a presence (John Sweeney was at Davos), and there was no one there from the National Organization for Women. Even Noam Chomsky, who said the forum "offers opportunities of unparalleled importance to bring together popular forces," sent only his regrets. Public Citizen had two people in Porto Alegre, but their star, Lori Wallach, was in Davos.

"Where are the Americans?" people asked, waiting in coffee lines and around Internet linkups. There were many theories. Some blamed the media: The American press wasn't covering the event. Of 1,500 journalists registered, maybe ten were American, and more than half of those were from Independent Media Centers. Some blamed Bush. The forum was held a week after his inauguration, which meant that most US activists were too busy protesting the theft of the election to even think about going to Brazil. Others blamed the French. Many groups didn't know about the event at all, in part because international outreach was done mainly by ATTAC, which, Christophe Aguiton acknowledged, needs "better links with the Anglo-Saxon world."

Most, however, blamed the Americans themselves. "Part of it is simply a reflection of US parochialism," said Peter Marcuse, a professor of urban planning at Columbia University and a speaker at the forum. It's a familiar story: If it doesn't happen in the United States, if it isn't in English, if it's not organized by American groups, it can't be all that important—let alone be the sequel to the Battle of Seattle.

Last year, *New York Times* columnist Thomas Friedman wrote from Davos, "Every year at the World Economic Forum there is a star or theme that stands out"—the dotcoms, the Asian crisis. Last year according to Friedman, the star of Davos was "Seattle." Porto Alegre had a star as well; it was, without question, "democracy": What happened to it? How do we get it back? And why isn't there more of it within the conference itself?

In workshops and on panels, globalization was defined as a mass transfer of wealth and knowledge from public to private—through the patenting of life and seeds, the privatization of water and the concentrated ownership of agricultural lands. Having this conversation in Brazil meant that these issues were not presented as shocking new inventions of a hitherto unheard-of phenomenon called "globalization"—as is often the case in the West—but as part of the continuum of colonization, centralization and loss of self-determination that began more than five centuries ago.

This latest stage of market integration has meant that power and decision-making are now delegated to points even farther away from the places where the effects of those decisions are felt at the same time that ever-greater financial burdens are off-loaded to cities and towns. Real power has moved from local to state, from state to national, from national to international, until finally representative democracy means voting for politicians every few years who use that mandate to transfer national powers to the WTO and the IMF.

In response to this democratic crisis, the forum set out to sketch the possible alternatives—but before long, some rather profound questions emerged. Is this a movement trying to impose its own, more humane brand of globalization, with taxation of global finance and more democracy and transparency in international governance? Or is it a movement against centralization and the delegation of power on principle, one as critical of left-wing, one-size-fits-all ideology as of the recipe for McGovernment churned out at forums like Davos (cut taxes, privatize, deregulate and wait for the trickle-down)? It's fine to cheer for the possibility of another world—but is the goal one specific other world ("our" world, some might say) or is it, as the Zapatistas put it, "a world with the possibility of many worlds in it"?

On these questions there was no consensus. Some groups, those with ties to political parties, seemed to be pushing for a united international organization or party and wanted the forum to issue an official manifesto that could form a governmental blueprint. Others, those working outside traditional political channels and often using direct action, were advocating less a unified vision than a universal right to self-determination and diversity: agricultural diversity, cultural diversity and, yes, even political diversity.

Atila Roque was one of the people who argued forcefully that the forum should not try to issue a single set of political demands. "We are trying to break the uniformity of thought, and you can't do that by putting forward another uniform way of thinking. Honestly, I don't miss the time when we were all in the Communist Party. We can achieve a higher degree of consolidation of the agendas, but I don't think civil society should be trying to organize itself into a party."

In the end, the conference did not speak in one voice; there was no single official statement (though there were dozens of unofficial ones). Instead of sweeping blueprints for political change, there were glimpses of local democratic alternatives. The Landless Peasants Movement took delegates on day trips to reappropriated farmland used for sustainable agriculture. And then there was the living alternative of Porto Alegre itself. The city has become a showcase of participatory democracy studied around the world. In Porto Alegre, democracy isn't a polite matter of casting ballots; it's a contact sport, carried out in sprawling town hall meetings. The centerpiece of the Workers Party's platform is something called "the participatory budget," an initiative that gives residents, through a network of neighborhood councils and a shadow city council, a direct say in such decisions as how much of the municipal budget should go to sanitation versus transportation.

"This is a city that is developing a new model of democracy in which people don't just hand over control to the state," British author Hilary Wainwright said at the forum. "The challenge is, how do we extend that to a national and global level?"

Perhaps by transforming the anticorporate, antiglobalization movement into a pro-democracy movement that defends the rights of local communities to plan and manage their schools, their water and their ecology. In Porto Alegre, the most convincing responses to the international failure of representative democracy seemed to be this radical form of local participatory democracy, in the cities and towns where the abstractions of global rule become day-to-day issues of homelessness, water contamination, exploding prisons and cash-starved schools. Of course, this has to take place within a context of national and international standards and resources. But what seemed to be emerging organically out of the World Social Forum (despite the best efforts of some of the organizers) was not a movement for a single global government but a vision for an increasingly connected international network of very local initiatives, each built on direct democracy.

Democracy was a topic that came up not only on the panels and in workshops but also in the hallways and in raucous late-night meetings at the youth campground. Here the subject was not how to democratize world governance or even municipal decision-making—but something closer to home: the yawning "democratic deficit" of the World Social Forum itself.

On one level the forum was extraordinarily open: Anyone who wanted to could attend as a delegate, with no restrictions on numbers of attendees. And any group that wanted to run a workshop—alone or with another group—simply had to get a title to the organizing committee before the program was printed.

But there were sometimes sixty of these workshops going on simultaneously, while the main-stage events, where there was an opportunity to address more than 1,000 delegates at a time, were dominated not by activists but by politicians and academics. Some gave rousing presentations, while others seemed painfully detached: After traveling eighteen hours or more to attend the forum, few needed to be told that "globalization is a space of dispute." It didn't help that these panels were dominated by men in their fifties, too many of them white. Nicola Bullard, deputy director of Bangkok's Focus on the Global South, half-joked that the opening press conference "looked like the Last Supper: twelve men with an average age of 52." And it probably wasn't a great idea that the VIP room, an enclave of invitation-only calm and luxury, was made of glass. This in-your-face two-tiering amid all the talk of people power began to grate around the time the youth campsite ran out of toilet paper.

The griping about a "coup d'état of the French intellectuals" was symbolic of a larger problem. The organizational structure of the forum was so opaque that it was nearly impossible to figure out how decisions were made or to find ways to question those decisions. There were no open plenaries and no chance to vote on the structure of future events. In the absence of a transparent process, fierce NGO brand wars were waged behind the scenes—about whose stars would get the most airtime, who would get access to the press and who would be seen as the true leaders of this movement.

By the third day, frustrated delegates began to do what they do best: Protest. There were marches and manifestoes—a half-dozen at least. Beleaguered forum organizers found themselves charged with everything from reformism to racism. The Anti-Capitalist Youth contingent accused them of ignoring the important role direct action played in building the movement. Their manifesto condemned the conference as "a ruse" using the mushy language of democracy to avoid a more divisive discussion of class. The PSTU, a breakaway faction of the Workers Party, began interrupting speeches about the possibility of another world with loud chants of: "Another world is *not* possible, unless you smash capitalism and bring in socialism!" (It sounded much better in Portuguese.)

Some of this criticism was unfair. The forum accommodated an extraordinary range of views, and it was precisely this diversity that made conflicts inevitable. By bringing together groups with such different ideas about power—unions, political parties, NGOs, anarchist street protesters and agrarian reformers—the World Social Forum only made visible the tensions that are always just under the surface of these fragile coalitions.

But other questions were legitimate and have implications that reach far beyond a one-week conference. How are decisions made in this movement of movements? Who, for instance, decides which "civil society representatives" go behind the barbed wire at Davos—while protesters are held back with water cannons outside? If Porto Alegre was the anti-Davos, why were some of the most visible faces of opposition "dialoguing" *in* Davos?

With a sweeping new round of WTO negotiations set for the fall, and the Free Trade Area of the Americas (FTAA) being negotiated in April, these questions about process are suddenly urgent. How do we determine whether the goal is to push for "social clauses" on labor and environmental issues in international agreements or to try to shoot down the agreements altogether? This debate—academic at previous points because there was so much resistance to social clauses from business—is now very real. US industry leaders, including

Caterpillar and Boeing, are actively lobbying for the linking of trade with labor and environmental clauses, not because they want to raise standards but because these links are viewed as the key to breaking the Congressional stalemate over fast-track trade negotiating authority. By pushing for social clauses, are unions and environmentalists unwittingly helping the advancement of these negotiations, a process that will also open the door to privatization of such services as water and more aggressive protections of drug patents? Should the goal be to add onto these trade agreements or take entire sections out—water, agriculture, food safety, drug patents, education, healthcare? Walden Bello, executive director of Focus on the Global South, is unequivocal on this point. "The WTO is unreformable," he said at the forum, "and it is a horrible waste of money to push for reform. Labor and environmental clauses will just empower an already too-powerful organization."

But that is not the strategy leading up to the Summit of the Americas in Quebec. Several large labor organizations and NGOs have taken government money to organize a parallel People's Summit during the official week of meetings, and have yet to issue clear statements on the FTAA. Not surprisingly, there were tensions about these issues at the forum, with those favoring direct action accusing the People's Summit organizers of helping to make the closed FTAA process appear open to "civil society"—perhaps just the public relations gloss Bush needs to secure fast track.

There is a serious debate to be had over strategy and process, but it's difficult to see how it will unfold without bogging down a movement whose greatest strength so far has been its agility. Anarchist groups, though fanatical about process, tend to resist efforts to structure or centralize the movement. The International Forum on Globalization—the brain trust of the North American side of the movement—lacks transparency in its decision-making and isn't accountable to a broad membership. Meanwhile, NGOs that might otherwise collaborate often compete with one another for publicity and funding. And traditional membership-based political structures like parties and unions have been reduced to bit players in these wide webs of activism.

Perhaps the real lesson of Porto Alegre is that democracy and accountability need to be worked out first on more manageable scales—within local communities and coalitions and inside individual organizations. Without this foundation, there's not much hope for a satisfying democratic process when 10,000 activists from wildly different backgrounds are thrown in a room together. What has become clear is that if the one "pro" this disparate coalition can get behind is "pro-democracy," then democracy within the movement must become a high priority. The Porto Alegre Call for Mobilization clearly states that "we challenge the elite and their undemocratic processes, symbolized by the World Economic Forum in Davos." Most delegates agreed that it simply won't do to scream "Elitist!" from a glass house—or from a glass VIP lounge.

Despite the moments of open revolt, the World Social Forum ended on as euphoric a note as it began. There was cheering and chanting, the loudest of which came when the organizing committee announced that Porto Alegre would host the forum again next year. The plane from Porto Alegre to São Paulo on January 30 was filled with delegates dressed head-to-toe in conference swag—T-shirts, baseball hats, mugs, bags—all bearing the utopian slogan: Another World Is Possible. Not uncommon, perhaps, after a conference, but it did strike me as noteworthy that a couple sitting in the seats across from me were still wearing their WSF name tags. It was as if they wanted to hang on to that dream world, however imperfect, for as long as they could before splitting up to catch connecting flights to Newark, Paris, Mexico City, absorbed in a hive of scurrying businesspeople, duty-free Gucci bags and CNN stock news.

Calls to Action from Social Movements

The international meetings of social movements are some of the widest articulations that have occurred in the World Social Forum. Each one produced a declaration that had an important role as a reference for the battles of the global movement.

**World Social Forum 2001
Porto Alegre, Brazil
Call for Mobilization**

Social forces from around the world have gathered here at the World Social Forum in Porto Alegre. Unions and NGOs, movements and organizations, intellectuals and artists, together we are building a great alliance to create a new society, different from the dominant logic wherein the free market and money are considered the only measure of worth. Davos represents the concentration of wealth, the globalization of poverty and the destruction of our earth. Porto Alegre represents the hope that a new world is possible, where human beings and nature are the center of our concern.

We are part of a movement which has grown since Seattle. We challenge the elite and their undemocratic processes, symbolized by the World Economic Forum in Davos. We came to share our experiences, build our solidarity, and demonstrate our total rejection of the neoliberal policies of globalization.

We are women and men, farmers, workers, unemployed, professionals, students, blacks, and indigenous peoples, coming from the South and from the North, committed to struggle for peoples' rights, freedom, security, employment and education. We are fighting against the hegemony of finance, the destruction of our cultures, the monopolization of knowledge, mass media, and communication, the degradation of nature, and the destruction of the quality of life by multinational corporations and anti-democratic policies. Participative democratic experiences—like that of Porto Alegre—show us that a concrete alternative is possible. We reaffirm the supremacy of human, ecological, and social rights over the demands of finance and investors.

At the same time that we strengthen our movements, we resist the global elite and work for equity, social justice, democracy and security for everyone, without distinction. Our methodology and alternatives stand in stark contrast to the destructive policies of neoliberalism.

Globalization reinforces a sexist and patriarchal system. It increases the feminization of poverty and exacerbates all forms of violence against women. Equality between women and men is central to our struggle. Without this, another world will never be possible.

Neoliberal globalization increases racism, continuing the veritable genocide of centuries of slavery and colonialism which destroyed the bases of black African civilizations. We call on all movements to be in solidarity with African peoples in the continent and outside, in defense of their rights to land, citizenship, freedom, peace, and equality, through the reparation of historical and social debts. The slave trade and slavery are crimes against humanity.

We express our special recognition and solidarity with indigenous peoples in their historic struggle against genocide and ethnocide and in defense of their rights, natural resources, culture, autonomy, land, and territory.

Neoliberal globalization destroys the environment, health, and people's living environment. Air, water, land, and peoples have become commodities. Life and health must be recognized as fundamental rights which must not be subordinated to economic policies.

The external debt of the countries of the South has been repaid several times over. Illegitimate, unjust, and fraudulent, it functions as an instrument of domination, depriving people of their fundamental human rights with the sole aim of increasing international usury. We demand its unconditional cancellation and the reparation of historical, social, and ecological debts as immediate steps toward a definitive resolution of the crisis this debt provokes.

Financial markets extract resources and wealth from communities and nations, and subject national economies to the whims of speculators. We call for the closure of tax havens and the introduction of taxes on financial transactions.

Privatization is a mechanism for transferring public wealth and natural resources to the private sector. We oppose all forms of privatization of natural resources and public services.

We call for the protection of access to resources and public goods necessary for a decent life.

Multinational corporations organize global production with massive unemployment, low wages, and unqualified labor and by refusing to recognise the fundamental workers' rights as defined by the ILO [International Labor Organization]. We demand the genuine recognition of the right to organize and negotiate for unions, and new rights for workers to face the globalization strategy. While goods and money are free to cross borders, the restrictions on the movement of people exacerbate exploitation and repression. We demand an end to such restrictions.

We call for a trading system which guarantees full employment, food security, fair terms of trade, and local prosperity. Free trade is anything but free. Global trade rules ensure the accelerated accumulation of wealth and power by multinational corporations and the further marginalization and impoverishment of small farmers, workers, and local enterprises. We demand that governments respect their obligations to the international human rights instruments and multilateral environmental agreements. We call on people everywhere to support the mobilizations against the creation of the Free Trade Area of the Americas, an initiative which means the recolonization of Latin America and the destruction of fundamental social, economic, cultural, and environmental human rights.

The IMF, the World Bank and regional banks, the WTO, NATO, and other military alliances are some of the multilateral agents of neoliberal globalization. We call for an end to their interference in national policy. These institutions have no legitimacy in the eyes of the people and we will continue to protest against their measures.

Neoliberal globalization has led to the concentration of land ownership and favored corporate agricultural systems which are environmentally and socially destructive. It is based on export-oriented growth backed by large-scale infrastructure development, such as dams, which displaces people from their land and destroys their livelihoods. Their loss must be restored. We call for democratic agrarian reform. Land, water, and seeds must be in the hands of the peasants. We promote sustainable agricultural processes. Seeds and genetic stocks are the heritage of humanity. We demand that the use of transgenics [genetically modified organisms] and the patenting of life be abolished.

Militarism and corporate globalization reinforce each other to undermine democracy and peace. We totally refuse war as a way to solve conflicts and we oppose the arms race and the arms trade. We call for an end to the repression and criminalization of social protest. We condemn foreign military intervention in the internal affairs of our countries. We demand the lifting of embargoes and sanctions used as instruments of aggression and express our solidarity with those who suffer their consequences. We reject U.S. military intervention in Latin America through the Plan Colombia.

We call for a strengthening of alliances, and the implementation of common actions, on these principal concerns. We will continue to mobilize on them until the next Forum. We recognize that we are now in a better position to undertake the struggle for a different world, a world without misery, hunger, discrimination, and violence, with quality of life, equity, respect, and peace.

We commit ourselves to support all the struggles of our

common agenda to mobilize opposition to neoliberalism. Among our priorities for the coming months, we will mobilize globally against the

World Economic Forum, Cancun, Mexico, 26 and 27 February

Free Trade Area of the Americas, Buenos Aires, Argentina, 6–7 April, and Quebec City, Canada, 17–22 April

Asian Development Bank, Honolulu, May

G-8 Summit, Genoa, Italy, 15–22 July

IMF and World Bank Annual Meeting, Washington DC, USA, 28 September–4 October

World Trade Organisation, 5–9 November (Qatar?)

On April 17, we will support the international day of struggle against the importation of cheap agricultural products which create economic and social dumping, and the feminist mobilization against globalization in Genoa. We support the call for a world day of action against debt, to take place this year on July 20.

The proposals formulated are part of the alternatives being elaborated by social movements around the world. They are based on the principle that human beings and life are not commodities, and in the commitment to the welfare and human rights of all.

Our involvement in the World Social Forum has enriched understanding of each of our struggles and we have been strengthened. We call on all peoples around the world to join in this struggle to build a better future. The World Social Forum of Porto Alegre is a way to achieve peoples' sovereignty and a just world.

**World Social Forum 2002
Porto Alegre, Brazil
Call of Social Movements: Resistance to Neoliberalism,
War, and Militarism: For Peace and Social Justice**

1. In the face of continuing deterioration in the living conditions of people, we, social movements from all around the world, have come together in the tens of thousands at the second World Social Forum in Porto Alegre. We are here in spite of the attempts to break our solidarity. We come together again to continue our struggles against neoliberalism and war, to confirm the agreements of the last Forum, and to reaffirm that another world is possible.

2. We are diverse—women and men, adults and youth, indigenous peoples, rural and urban, workers and unemployed, homeless, the elderly, students, migrants, professionals, peoples of every creed, color, and sexual orientation. The expression of this diversity is our strength and the basis of our unity. We are a global solidarity movement, united in our determination to fight against the concentration of wealth, the proliferation of poverty and inequalities, and the destruction of our earth. We are living and constructing alternative systems, and using creative ways to promote them. We are building a large alliance from our struggles and resistance against a system based on sexism, racism, and violence, which privileges the interests of capital and patriarchy over the needs and aspirations of people.

3. This system produces a daily drama of women, children, and the elderly dying because of hunger, lack of health care, and preventable diseases. Families are forced to leave their homes because of wars, the impact of "big development," landlessness and environmental disasters, unemployment, attacks on public services, and the destruction of social solidarity. Both in the South and in the North, vibrant struggles and resistance to uphold the dignity of life are flourishing.

4. September 11 marked a dramatic change. After the terrorist attacks, which we absolutely condemn, as we condemn all other attacks on civilians in other parts of the world, the government of the United States and its allies launched a massive military operation. In the name of the "war against terrorism," civil and political rights are being attacked all over the world. The war against Afghanistan, in which terrorist methods are being used, is now being extended to other fronts. Thus there is the beginning of a permanent global war to cement the domination of the U.S. government and its allies. This war reveals another face of neoliberalism, a face that is brutal and unacceptable. Islam is being demonized, while racism and xenophobia are deliberately propagated. The mass media is actively taking part in this belligerent campaign, which divides the world into "good" and "evil." The opposition to the war is at the heart of our movement.

5. The situation of war has further destabilized the Middle East, providing a pretext for further repression of the Palestinian people. An urgent task of our movement is to

CALLS TO ACTION ◆ 189

mobilize solidarity for the Palestinian people and their struggle for self-determination as they face brutal occupation by the Israeli state. This is vital to collective security of all peoples in the region.

6. Further events also confirm the urgency of our struggles. In Argentina the financial and economic crisis caused by IMF structural adjustment and mounting debt precipitated a social and political crisis. This crisis generated spontaneous protests of the middle and working classes (repression which caused numerous deaths), failure of governments, and new alliances between different social groups. With the force of "*cacerolazos*" and "*piquetes,*" popular mobilizations have demanded their basic rights to food, jobs, and housing. We reject the criminalization of social movements in Argentina and the attacks against democratic rights and freedom. We also condemn the greed and the blackmail of multinational corporations supported by the governments of the rich countries.

7. The collapse of the multinational Enron exemplifies the bankruptcy of the casino economy and the corruption of businessmen and politicians, leaving workers without jobs and pensions. In developing countries this multinational engaged in fraudulent activities and its projects pushed people off their land and led to sharp increases in the price of water and electricity.

8. The United States government, in its efforts to protect the interests of big corporations, arrogantly walked away from negotiations on global warming, the antiballistic

missile treaty, the Convention on Biodiversity, the UN conference on racism and intolerance, and the talks to reduce the supply of small arms, proving once again that U.S. unilateralism undermines attempts to find multilateral solutions to global problems.

9. In Genoa the G-8 failed completely in its self-assumed task of global government. In the face of massive mobilization and resistance, they responded with violence and repression, denouncing as criminals those who dared to protest. But they failed to intimidate our movement.

10. All this is happening in the context of a global recession. The neoliberal economic model is destroying the rights, living conditions, and livelihoods of people. Using every means to protect their "share value," multinational companies lay off workers, slash wages, and close factories, squeezing the last dollar from the workers. Governments faced with this economic crisis respond by privatizing, cutting social-sector expenditures, and permanently reducing workers' rights. This recession exposes the fact that the neoliberal promise of growth and prosperity is a lie.

11. The global movement for social justice and solidarity faces enormous challenges: its fight for peace and collective security implies confronting poverty, discriminations, dominations, and the creation of an alternative sustainable society.

Social movements energetically condemn violence and militarism as a means of conflict resolution; the promotion of low-intensity conflicts and military operations in the Plan Colombia as part of the Andes regional initiative; the

Puebla Panama plan; the arms trade and higher military budgets; economic blockades against people and nations especially against Cuba and Iraq; and the growing repression against trade unions, social movements, and activists.

We support the trade unions and informal sector worker struggles as essential to maintain working and living conditions, the genuine right to organize, to go on strike, to negotiate collective agreements, and to achieve equality in wages and working conditions between women and men. We reject slavery and the exploitation of children. We support workers' struggles and the trade union fights against casualization, subcontracting of labor, and layoffs, and we demand new international rights for the employees of multinational companies and their affiliates, in particular the right to unionize and space for collective bargaining. Equally we support the struggles of farmers and peoples' organizations for their rights to a livelihood, and to land, forests, and water.

12. Neoliberal policies create tremendous misery and insecurity. They have dramatically increased the trafficking and sexual exploitation of women and children. Poverty and insecurity creates millions of migrants who are denied their dignity, freedom, and rights. We therefore demand the rights of free movement and physical integrity and the legal status of all migrants. We support the rights of indigenous peoples and the fulfillment of ILO article 169 ["Convention (No. 169) concerning Indigenous and Tribal Peoples in Independent Countries"] in national legal frameworks.

13. The external debt of the countries of the South has been repaid several times over. Illegitimate, unjust, and fraudulent, debt functions as an instrument of domination, depriving people of their fundamental human rights with the sole aim of increasing international usury. We demand unconditional cancellation of debt and the reparation of historical, social, and ecological debts. The countries demanding repayment of debt have engaged in exploitation of the natural resources and the traditional knowledge of the South.

14. Water, land, food, forests, seeds, culture, and people's identities are common assets of humanity for present and future generations. It is essential to preserve biodiversity. People have the right to safe and permanent food free from genetically modified organisms. Food sovereignty at the local, national, and regional level is a basic human right; in this regard, democratic land reforms and peasants' access to land are fundamental requirements.

15. The meeting in Doha confirmed the illegitimacy of the WTO. The adoption of the "development agenda" only defends corporate interests. By launching a new round, the WTO is moving closer to its goal of converting everything into a commodity. For us, food, public services, agriculture, health, and education are not for sale. Patenting must not to be used as a weapon against poor countries and peoples. We reject the patenting and trading of life forms. The WTO agenda is perpetuated at the continental level by regional free trade and investment agreements. By organizing protests such as the huge

demonstrations and plebiscites against FTAA, people have rejected these agreements as representing a recolonization and the destruction of fundamental social, economical, cultural, and environmental rights and values.

16. We will strengthen our movement through common actions and mobilizations for social justice, for the respect of rights and liberties, and for quality of life, equality, dignity, and peace. We are fighting for:

    - democracy: people have the right to know about and criticize the decisions of their own governments, especially with respect to dealings with international institutions. Governments are ultimately accountable to their people. While we support the establishment of electoral and participative democracy across the world, we emphasize the need for the democratization of states and societies and support the struggles against dictatorship.

    - the abolition of external debt and reparations.

    - a reducation in speculative activities: we demand the creation of specific taxes such as the Tobin Tax, and the abolition of tax havens.

    - the right to information.

    - women's rights and freedom from violence, poverty, and exploitation.

    - the end of war and militarism, foreign military bases and interventions, and the systematic escalation of violence. We choose to privilege negotiation and nonviolent conflict resolution. We affirm the right of all people to ask for international mediation, with the participation of independent actors from civil society.

- the rights of youth, their access to free public education and social autonomy, and the abolition of compulsory military service.
- the right to self-determination of all peoples, especially indigenous peoples.

In the years to come, we will organize collective mobilizations including, in 2002:

- 8 March: International Women's Day.
- 17 April: International Day of Peasants' Struggle.
- 1 May: Labour Day.
- 7 October: World Day for the Homeless.
- 12 October: Cry of the Excluded.
- 16 October: World Food Day.

Other global mobilizations will take place:

- 15–16 March: Barcelona (Spain), summit of the EU.
- 18–22 March: Monterrey (Mexico), United Nations Conference on Financing for Development.
- 17–18 May: Madrid (Spain), summit of Latin America, Caribbean, and Europe.
- May: Shanghai (China), Asia Development Bank Annual Meeting.

- 1 May: International day of action against militarism and for peace.
- end of May: Indonesia, fourth preparatory meeting for the World Summit on Sustainable Development.
- June: Roma (Italy), World Food Summit.
- 22–23 June: Sevilla (Spain) EU summit.
- July: Toronto and Calgary (Canada), G-8 summit.
- 22 July: USA campaign against Coca-Cola.
- September: Johannesburg (South Africa), Rio+10.
- September: Copenhagen (Denmark), Asia Europe Meeting (ASEM).
- October: Quito (Ecuador), "A New Integration is Possible," social continental forum.
- November: Cuba, 2nd Hemispheric meeting against FTAA.
- December: Copenhagen (Denmark), summit of EU.

In 2003:

- April: Buenos Aires (Argentina), summit of the FTAA.
- June: Thessaloniki, EU Summit.
- June: France, G-8.
- WTO, IMF, and World Bank will meet somewhere, sometime. And we will be there!

World Social Forum 2003
Porto Alegre, Brazil
Call of the World Social Movements

We are meeting in Porto Alegre in the shadow of a global crisis. The belligerent intentions of the United States government in its determination to launch a war on Iraq pose a grave threat to us all, and are a dramatic manifestation of the links between militarism and economic domination. At the same time, neoliberal globalization itself is in crisis: the threat of a global recession is ever present; corporate corruption scandals are daily news and expose the reality of capitalism.

Social and economic inequalities are growing, threatening the social structures of our societies and cultures, our rights, and our lives.

Biodiversity, air, water, forest, soil, and sea are used like commodities and are for sale.

All this threatens our common future.

We oppose this!

FOR OUR COMMON FUTURE

We are social movements that are fighting all around the world against neoliberal globalization, war, racism, castism, religious fanaticism, poverty, patriarchy, and all the forms of economical, ethnical, social, political, cultural, sexual, and gender discriminations and exclusions. We are all fighting for social justice, citizenship, participatory democracy, universal rights, and the right of peoples to decide their own future.

We stand for peace and international cooperation, for a sustainable society answering the needs of people for food, housing, health, education, information, water, energy, public transportation, and human rights.

We are in solidarity with the women engaged against social and patriarchal violence. We support the struggle of the peasants, workers, popular urban movements, and all those who are urgently threatened by being deprived of homes, jobs, land and their rights.

We have demonstrated in millions to say that another world is possible.

This has never been more true and more urgent.

NO WAR!

The social movements are against militarization, the increase of military bases and state repression that create countless refugees, and the criminalization of social movements and poor people.

We are against the war on Iraq; the attacks on the Palestinian, Chechen and Kurdish people; the wars in Afghanistan, in Colombia, and in Africa; and the growing threat of war on Korea. We oppose the economic and political aggression against Venezuela and the political and economic blockade by the U.S. government against Cuba. We are against all kinds of military and economic actions designed to impose the neoliberal model and undermine the sovereignty and peace of peoples around the world.

War—using military force to control people and strategic resources such as oil—has become a structural and permanent part of global domination. The United States government and its allies are imposing war as a more and more common solution for resolving conflicts. We also denounce the deliberate attempts made by imperialists to increase religious, ethnic, racist, tribal, and other tensions and strife all over the world in order to pursue their selfish interests.

[The] majority of public opinion around the world is opposed to the coming war on Iraq. We call on all social movements and progressive forces to support, participate in, and organize worldwide protests on February 15, 2003. These protests are already planned and coordinated by all those who oppose the war in over 30 major cities around the world.

DERAIL WTO

The World Trade Organization (WTO), the Free Trade Area of the Americas (FTAA), and a proliferation of regional and bilateral trade agreements, such as the Africa Growth and Opportunity Act (AGOA) and the proposed Central America free trade agreements, are used by multinational corporations to promote their interests, to dominate and control our economies, and to impose a development model which impoverishes our societies. In the name of trade liberalization, every aspect of life and nature is for sale and people are denied their basic rights. Agro-multinationals are trying to impose GMOs worldwide; people suffering from HIV/AIDS and other pandemics in Africa and elsewhere are denied access to cheap generic drugs. In addition, countries of the South are trapped in a never-ending cycle of debt that forces them to open up their markets and export their wealth.

In the coming year our campaigns against the WTO, the FTAA, and trade liberalization will grow in size and scope.

We will campaign to stop and reverse liberalization of agriculture, water, energy, public services and investment, and to reassert peoples' sovereignty over their societies, their resources, their cultures and knowledge and their economies.

We are in solidarity with the Mexican farmers who say "el campo no aguanta mas" ["the farmers are fed up"], and in the spirit of their struggles we will mobilize locally, nationally, and internationally to derail the WTO and the FTAA. We support the worldwide movement to fight for food sovereignty and against the neoliberal models of agriculture, food production, and distribution. In particular, we will organize mass protests around the world during the fifth ministerial meeting of the WTO in Cancun, Mexico, in September 2003 and during the ministerial meeting of the FTAA in Miami, USA, in October.

CANCEL THE DEBT

The full and unconditional cancellation of Third World debt constitutes a precondition to granting even the most basic human rights. We shall support any indebted country that would stop its external debt payment and would break its agreements with the IMF, especially the structural adjustment programs. Centuries of exploitation of the Third World people, their resources, and environment have given them the right to reparations. We ask, "Who owes whom?" These issues will be raised in the major campaigns being held in 2003, G-8 (Evian/June), WTO (Cancun/September), and the IMF and Word Bank annual meeting (Washington/September).

OPPOSING THE G-8

We call on all the social movements and progressive forces to be part of the mobilization to denounce the illegitimacy and to also reject the policies of the G-8 that will be meeting in Evian, France, 1–3 June 2003. This mobilization will be organized with an international gathering at Evian (France) that will include an alternative summit, an alternative camp, and a huge international demonstration.

WOMEN: PROMOTING EQUALITY

We are part of the actions promoted by women's movements on 8 March, which is the International Women's Day to fight against all forms of violence and patriarchy and for social and political equality.

IN SOLIDARITY

We call all progressive social forces, movements, and organizations across the world to stand in solidarity with those peoples such as the Palestinian, Venezuelan, Bolivian, and Cuban people (who fight against the U.S. embargo) and others who are facing extreme crisis and are fighting against imperialist hegemony at this very moment in time.

We call to the people. As we strongly believe that another world is possible, that other worlds are possible, because we have begun to build another world in our commitments, our struggles, and our international meetings, we are determined to go on and strengthen our unity against the war, against poverty, and for peace and social justice.

ENHANCE OUR INTERNATIONAL NETWORK

Last year during the World Social Forum in Porto Alegre we adopted a declaration that defines our aims, our struggles, and the ways we build our alliances. The spirit of this text is still living and will inspire our coming mobilizations.

Since then, the world has been changing very quickly and we feel the need to take a new step in our decision-making processes, in our coordinations and alliances—the need to promote a broad, radical, democratic, plural, internationalist, feminist, nondiscriminatory, and anti-imperialist agenda.

We now want to build a framework articulating our analyses and commitments to our mobilizations. This requires the active participation of all the movements, keeping in mind that the social forums are independent from governments and political parties (as given in the WSF Charter of Principles) and maintaining a respect for their autonomy. This framework would be strengthened by a variety of social actors contributing and sharing their experiences and concrete social practices. Further, this would be in accordance with the different forms of political expression and organization of the social movements and with regard to the diversity of ideologies and cultures.

We feel the need to create a network of movements that is responsive, flexible, and sustainable, yet is also broad and transparent. Its responsibilities should be to enrich and feed the process, to promote its diversity, and to assume the necessary degree of coordination. The aims of the network will be to enhance the engagement of movements around the world in a deeper political debate, to facilitate common action, and to strengthen the initiative of concrete actors fighting for social interests. Its work should be both horizontal and effective.

To this end we propose to build a contact group as a resource and tool for our international mobilizations; it will prepare meetings and promote debate and democracy through a website and mailing lists. This contact group will be established for a period of between six and twelve months and it will draw on the past experience of the supporters of the network of social and popular movements that are based in Brazil.

This arrangement is transitional to ensure continuity. The main task of this provisory group is to facilitate debate so that the social movements around the world define concrete procedures to work together. It is an ongoing process. A first review of the new contact group will take place at meetings of the network of social movements during the mass mobilization against the WTO in Cancun in September 2003. A second review, again in assemblies of the network of social movements, will follow during the WSF meeting that is expected to be held in India in 2004.

Among other things, the reviews will consider the effectiveness of the coordination and seek new ways to enhance it. They will also consider how to proceed from one year to the next, and how to include national and regional movements and thematic campaigns. In the meantime, we need a large debate among organizations, campaigns, and networks to articulate the proposals for a more permanent and representative structure.

In the months to come we will have many occasions to experiment, improve, and build this process through our campaigns and mobilizations.

World Social Forum 2004
Mumbai, India
Call of Social Movements and Mass Organizations

We the social movements united in assembly in the city of Mumbai, India, share the struggles of the people of India and all Asians. We reiterate our opposition to the neoliberal system, which generates economic, social, and environmental crises and produces war. Our mobilization against war and deep social and economic injustices has served to reveal the true face of neoliberalism.

We are united here to organize the resistance against capitalism and to find alternatives. Our resistance began in Chiapas, Seattle, and Genoa, and led to a massive worldwide mobilization against the war in Iraq on 15th February 2003 which condemned the strategy of global, ongoing war implemented by the United States government and its allies. It is this resistance that led to the victory over the WTO in Cancun.

The occupation of Iraq showed the whole world the existing links between militarism and the economic domination of the multinational corporations. Moreover, it also justified the reasons for our mobilization.

As social movements and mass organizations, we reaffirm our commitment to fight neoliberal globalization, imperialism, war, racism, the caste system, cultural imperialism, poverty, patriarchy, and all forms of discrimination—economic, social, political, ethnic, gender, sexual—including that of sexual orientation and gender identity. We are also against all kinds of discrimination to persons with different capacities and fatal illnesses such as AIDS.

We struggle for social justice, access to natural resources—land, water, and seeds—human and citizens' rights, paticipative democracy, the rights of workers of both genders as guaranteed in international treaties, women's rights, and also the people's right to self-determination. We are partisans of peace and international cooperation, and we promote sustainable societies that are able to guarantee access to public services and basic goods. At the same time, we reject social and patriarchal violence against women.

We call for a mass mobilization on 8th March, International Women's Day.

We fight all forms of terrorism, including state terrorism. At the same time we are opposed to the use of terrorism, which criminalizes popular movements and restricts civil activists. The so-called law against terrorism restricts civil rights and democratic freedom all over the world.

We vindicate the struggle of peasants, workers, popular urban movements, and all people under threat of losing their homes, jobs, land, or rights. We also vindicate the struggle to reverse privatization in order to protect common public goods, as is happening with pensions and social security in Europe. The victory of the massive mobilization of the Bolivian people in defense of their natural resources, democracy, and sovereignty testifies to the strength and potential of our movements. Simultaneously, peasants across the globe are struggling against multinationals and neoliberal corporate agricultural policies, demanding sovereignty over food and democratic land reform.

We call for unity with all peasants on 17th April, International Day of Peasants' Struggles.

We identify with the struggle of the mass movements and popular organizations in India, and together with them we condemn the political and ideological forces which promote violence, sectarianism, exclusion, and nationalism based on religion and ethnicity. We condemn the threats, arrests, torture, and assassinations of social activists who organized communities in order to struggle for global justice. We also denounce discrimination based on caste, class, religion, gender, sexual orientation, and gender identity. We condemn the perpetuation of violence and oppression against women through cultural, religious, and traditional discriminatory practices.

We support the efforts of mass movements and popular organizations in India and Asia which promote the struggle for justice, equality and human rights, especially that of the Dalits, Adivasis, and the most oppressed and repressed sectors of society. The neoliberal policy of the Indian government aggravated the marginalization and social oppression which the Dalits have suffered historically.

For all these reasons we support the struggle of all the marginalized throughout the world, and urge everyone worldwide to join the call of the Dalits for a day of mobilization for social inclusion.

As an escape from its crisis of legitimacy, global capitalism is using force and war in order to maintain an anti-popular order. We demand that the governments put a stop to militarism, war, and military spending, and demand the closure of U.S. military bases because they are a risk and threat to humanity and life on earth. We have to follow the example of the people of Puerto Rico who forced the U.S. to close its base in Vieques. The opposition to global warfare remains our main object of mobilization around the world.

We call on all citizens of the world to mobilize simultaneously on 20th March in an international day of protest against war and the occupation of Iraq imposed by the United States, Great Britain, and the Allied Forces.

In each country, the antiwar movements are developing their own consensus and tactics in order to guarantee as wide a participation and mobilization as possible. We demand the immediate withdrawal of all occupying troops and support the right of the Iraqi people to self-determination and sovereignity, as well as their right to reparation for all the damages caused by the embargo and war.

The struggle against terrorism not only acts as a pretext for continuing the war and occupation of Iraq and Afghanistan, but is also being used to threaten and attack the global community. At the same time, the U.S. is maintaining a criminal embargo against Cuba, and destabilizing Venezuela.

We call upon all people to give maximum support this year to the mobilization for the Palestinian people, especially on 30th March, Palestinian Land Day, against the building of the wall of apartheid.

We denounce imperialist forces that are generating religious, ethnic, racial and tribal conflicts in order to further their own interests, increasing the suffering of the people and multiplying the hate and violence between them. More than 80 percent of the ongoing conflicts in the world are internal and especially affect African and Asian communities.

We denounce the unsustainable situation of debt in poor countries of the world, and the coercive use of debt by governments, multinational corporations, and international financial institutions. We strongly demand the total and unconditional cancellation and rejection of the illegitimate debts of the Third World. As a preliminary condition for the satisfaction of the fundamental economic, social, cultural, and political rights, we also demand the restitution of the long-standing plunder of the Third World. We especially support the struggle of the African peoples and their social movements.

Once again we raise our voices against the G-8 Summit and the meetings of the IMF and World Bank, which bear the greatest responsibility for the plunder of entire communities.

We reject the imposition of regional and bilateral free-trade agreements such as FTAA, NAFTA, CAFTA, AGOA, NEPAD, Euro-Med, AFTA, and ASEAN.

We are millions of persons united in the struggle against our common enemy: the WTO. The indigenous people are struggling against patents on all kinds of life-forms and the theft of biodiversity, water, and land. We are united in fighting the privatization of public services and common goods.

We call upon everybody to mobilize for the right to water as a source of life that cannot be privatized. We are endeavoring to recover control over public common goods and natural resources, previously privatized and given to transnational enterprises and the private sector.

In the victory at Cancun, the death of Lee* symbolized the suffering of millions of peasants and poor people all over the world who are excluded by the "free market." His immolation is a symbol for our struggle against the WTO. This proves

---

* Kun Hai Lee was a South Korean farmer who committed suicide in Cancún to protest the WTO's agriculture policy.

our determination to oppose any attempt to revive the WTO.

WTO out of agriculture, food, health, water, education, natural resources, and common goods!

With this determination in mind, we call upon all the social movement and mass organizations of the world to join the mobilization in Hong Kong or in any other place where the WTO ministerial will be held. Let us join our efforts to struggle against privatization and in defense of common goods: environment, agriculture, water, health, public services and education.

In order to achieve our objectives, we reiterate our strong desire to reinforce the network of social movements and our capacity for struggle.

GLOBALIZE THE STRUGGLE! GLOBALIZE THE HOPE!

Organizations and Entities Involved in the Global Movement

50 Years Is Enough

This coalition of two hundred North American organizations fights for the transformation of the IMF and World Bank. Its demands were formulated after a fifteen-month consultation with representatives in thirteen Asian, African, Latin American, and Caribbean countries.

Contact: 50years@50years.org
Web site: www.50years.org

ABONG—Brazilian Association of NGOs

Created in 1991, ABONG acts as a collective representative of NGOs together with the state and other civil society actors. Its principal objective is to promote interchange between the NGOs acting to strengthen citizen participation in the fight for social rights and democracy. Currently, it has 251 member organizations.

Contact: abong@uol.com.br
Web site: www.abong.org.br

AFL-CIO—American Federation of Labor–Congress of Industrial Organizations

The main labor union federation in the United States, it has sixty-five national and international unions, currently representing thirteen million members.

Contact: feedback@aflcio.org
Web site: www.aflcio.org

AFM—Articulación Feminista Marcosur

Formed in September 2000, beginning at the Fourth World Conference on Women (Beijing+5), by organizations in Uruguay, Brazil, Chile, Paraguay, Argentina, Bolivia, and Peru, AFM seeks to strengthen the articulation spaces between social movements, and to reinforce and influence these spheres with a feminist presence, for society in general.

Contact: mujeresdelsur@mujersur.org.uy
Web site: www.mujeresdelsur.org.uy

AIC—Alternative Information Center

This Israeli-Palestinian organization works to disseminate information, research, and political analyses of the two societies, as well as about the Israel–Palestine conflict. It promotes cooperation between Palestinians and Israelis based on the values of social justice, solidarity, and community involvement.

Contact: aic@alt-info.org
Web site: www.alternativenews.org

AIDC—Alternative Information and Development Centre

This NGO works in the context of globalization together with popular and social movements in South Africa and the region, seeking economic and social transformation. Its principal areas of action: external debt, international trade, finances, and macroeconomic policies.

Contact: info@aidc.org.za
Web site: aidc.org.za

ALAI—Latin American Information Agency

This organization and news agency is focused on the democratization of information, enforcement of human rights, and participation of social movements in Latin America's development.

Contact: info@alainet.org
Web site: www.alainet.org

Alternatives

This organization promotes solidarity, justice, and equality among individuals of the North and South. It works in more than thirty-five countries and supports initiatives of community movements through respect for economic, social, and political rights.

Contact: alternatives@alternatives.ca
Web site: www.alternatives.ca

Amnesty International

This is a global movement independent of governments, political ideology, and economic or religious interests that seeks international recognition of human rights. It has 1.5 million members in 150 countries.

Contact: Country-specific contacts available through Web site
Web site: www.amnesty.org

APC—Association for Progressive Communications

Officially founded in 1990, this group seeks to connect civil society organizations that have the same objectives but have not been communicating with each other. It established an international network that gave assistance to and collaborated for empowerment of groups and individuals that work for peace, human rights, development, and environmental protection.

Contact: webeditor@apc.org
Web site: www.apc.org

Arab NGO Network for Development

This network is active in the fields of social development, human rights, gender, and environment, and has a presence in twelve Arab countries. Its objective is to empower Arab society and strengthen the concepts of democracy, civil society, sustainable human development, and social justice, based in solidarity, cooperation, and opposition to violence.

Contact: webmaster@annd.org
Web site: www.annd.org

ATTAC—Association for the Taxation of Financial Transactions for the Aid of Citizens

Founded in June 1998 in France, this organization fights for implementation of taxes on all financial transactions; against offshore tax havens and antisocial policies of organizations such as the IMF, World Bank, WTO, and OECD; for the democratization of control of pension funds; and for the creation of new regulatory instruments and financial controls on national and international levels. Currently, the organization is present in 33 countries in Europe, Africa, and Latin America.

Contact: webmaster@attac.org
Web site: www.attac.org

CADTM—Committee for the Abolition of the Third World Debt

Founded in 1990 in Belgium, this committee works in different countries in Africa and Europe. It combines analyses of the debt problem with citizen mobilization, coordinating national movements that work on the issue of external debt. It also runs the campaign "Abolish the Debt to Free Development."

Contact: info@cadtm.org
Web site: www.cadtm.org

Caritas Internacionalis

The first Caritas was born in Freiburg, Germany, in 1897. In December 1951, it formed the constituent General Assembly of Caritas Internationalis. Currently it is a federation of 162 Catholic assistance, development, and social service organizations that work to build a better world for the poor and oppressed.

Contact: caritas.internationalis@caritas.va
Web site: www.caritas.org

CBJP—Brazilian Peace and Justice Commission

The CBJP has its origins in a commission created in Rome following the Vatican II Council. In 1967, Pope Paul VI created the Pontifical Peace and Justice Commission, with representatives from all continents. In October 1969, the commission was launched in Brazil and has as a mission to concretize the principles enunciated in the encyclical *Populorum progressio*.

Contact: cbjp@cbjp.org.br
Web site: www.cbjp.org.br

CCSCS—Coordination of National Labor Unions of the Southern Cone

Created in Buenos Aires in 1986, it coordinates and articulates national labor unions in the Southern Cone. Its primary objectives were to defend democracy and human rights, fight against authoritarian regimes that still existed in the region (Chile and Paraguay), and organize region-wide action against the external debt and its impacts on economies in countries within the Southern Cone. In 1990, it began to monitor the Mercosur integration process.

Contact: info@ccscs.org
Web site: www.ccscs.org

CEAAL—Education Council of Latin American Adults

Created in 1982, this council includes 195 organizations in 21 Latin American and Caribbean countries. It promotes popular education for the democratic transformation of society and to win peace and human rights.

Contact: ceaal@laneta.apc.org
Web site: www.ceaal.org

CIDSE—International Cooperation for Development and Solidarity

Established in 1967, CIDSE coordinates Catholic aid agencies that work on campaigns and support initiatives for the development of countries in the South.

Contact: postmaster@cidse.org
Web site: www.cidse.org

CIVES—Brazilian Association of Businesspeople for Citizenship

Founded at the end of the 1980s by a group of businesspeople committed to the social question in Brazil, this organization's principal objectives are to provide incentives for and to promote participation of businesspeople in politics, to establish a bridge between progressive parties, especially the Workers' Party and the business class, to promote a democratic, participative, and transparent relationship between the state and society, and to construct and promote a new ethic in the relationship between capital and labor.

Contact: cives@cives.org.br
Web site: www.cives.org.br

CLACSO—Latin American Council of Social Sciences

Founded in 1967 by Latin American social scientists, it is a network of around 5,000 researchers spread across 122 member centers in Latin America and the Caribbean. It has as an objective to promote research, discussion, and academic diffusion in diverse fields of social sciences.

Contact: clacso@clacso.edu.ar
Web site: www.clacso.org

CLC—Canadian Labour Congress

A federation of unions in Canada, it represents 2.5 million organized workers in the country.

Contact: international@clc-ctc.ca
Web site: www.clc-ctc.ca

CNI—Indigenous National Congress of Mexico

This is a space of active participation of authorities, peoples, and indigenous organizations that have as an objective the search for a new relationship between indigenous groups and the Mexican state and national society to construct peace with justice and dignity.

> Contact: ceacatl@laneta.apc.org
> Web site: www.laneta.apc.org/cni

Conaie—Confederation of Indigenous Nationalities of Ecuador

An autonomous organization that fights for the rights of indigenous people in Ecuador and supports the construction of a plural-national state. This confederation also fights for specific rights of the community and against government policies contrary to the rights of indigenous people.

> Contact: conaie@ecuanex.net.ec
> Web site: conaie.org

Corpwatch

Based in San Francisco, it works through education and mobilization for a globalization directed toward human rights and environmental justice. It had an important role in the pressure against Nike and in the Seattle protests.

> Contact: corpwatch@corpwatch.org
> Web site: www.corpwatch.org

Cry of the Excluded

Born in Brazil in 1995 as the continuation of the Campaign of Fraternity, it was organized initially by Catholic social service organizations. Over time, social movements, unions, and NGOs became involved in the process. It expanded to Latin America in 1999, and into the Americas in 2000. It demands agrarian reform, changes in economic policies, demarcation and protection of indigenous lands, respect for the environment, an end to dependence, and cancellation of external debts.

Contact: gritoexcluidos@uol.com.br
Web site: gritodosexcluidos.com.br

CSA—Continental Social Alliance

A forum of organizations and progressive social movements of the Americas, this alliance was created in 1999 with the objective of exchanging information, defining strategies, and promoting joint actions for alternative and democratic development.

Contact: asc@laneta.apc.org
Web site: www.asc-hsa.org

CTA—Argentine Workers' Central

Central labor union created in 1992, it is founded on direct affiliation, full democracy, and political autonomy. Its objective is to provide instruments for a new union model that contributes to change Argentinean society.

Contact: secgeneral@cta.org.ar
Web site: www.cta.org.ar

CUT—Workers' Central Union

Founded in August 1983, this union was the fruit of a broad movement fighting for Brazilian workers. It arose out of the opposition to the paternalistic and corporate-oriented labor relations and union structure. It characterizes itself through its search for new forms of relationships and participation of workers in the day-to-day work of the unions.

Contact: faleconosco@cut.org.br
Web site: www.cut.org.br

Dawn—Development Alternatives with Women for a New Era

This network was launched in 1984 when a group of feminists in the South organized workshops in the NGOs' parallel forum to the UN World Conference on Women in Nairobi, debating macroeconomic themes linked to the women's movement agenda on development and offering analysis from the perspective of women in the South.

Contact: admin@dawn.org.fj
Web site: www.dawn.org.fj

Doctors Without Borders

Created in 1971 by a group of young doctors and journalists who worked as volunteers in Biafra and Nigeria at the end of the 1960s, it sought primarily to provide health care for those most in need. The following year, the group made its first intervention in Nicaragua after an earthquake devastated the country. Currently, more than ten thousand professionals work in the organization in around ninety countries.

Web site: www.doctorswithoutborders.org

ENDA–TM—Environmental Development Action in the Third World

ENDA–TM was founded in 1972 in Dakar, Senegal, as a program that works together with the United Nations, the African Institute for Economic Development and Planning, and the Swedish Organization for International Development. Beginning in 1978, ENDA was constituted as an international organization composed of autonomous entities and an executive secretary responsible for coordinating its work.

Contact: enda@enda.sn
Web site: www.enda.sn

ETUC—European Trade Union Confederation

Created in 1973, this confederation intends to offer a counterweight to the economic forces of European integration. After the changes in Eastern Europe, a large number of new unions joined. Currently ETUC has seventy-six national centers in thirty-four countries, with sixty million members.

Contact: etuc@etuc.org
Web site: www.etuc.org

FIDH—International Federation for Human Rights

Created in 1922, this federation was persecuted by Nazism and had a central role in the creation of the Human Rights Declaration. Currently, it is a network of 141 integrated organizations for human rights in 90 countries.

Web site: www.fidh.org

Focus on the Global South

Dedicated to the study of the impact of neoliberal globalization on the Asia-Pacific region, this group promotes ideas of deglobalization and subsidiarity and the formation of local economic systems centered on the basic needs of the poorest. It provides assistance for local development projects in Thailand, the Philippines, India, and Bangladesh, and sponsors regional programs on democracy and development, cultural answers to globalization, and models for new industrialization. It also specializes in analysis of international institutions.

Contact: admin@focusweb.org
Web site: focusweb.org

Friends of the Earth International

Founded in 1971 by four organizations in France, Switzerland, Britain, and the United States, it is currently present in 70 countries. Its objective is to protect the environment and establish sustainable societies, as well as to promote campaigns about hot issues such as nuclear energy and whaling.

Web site: www.foei.org

Friends of the River Narmada

A coalition of individuals and organizations involved in the fight against the construction of huge dams in the Narmada River in India, it is also pledged to the global fight for social justice and the environment.

Contact: patrick@irn.org
Web site: www.narmada.org

Global Exchange

Global Exchange is a U.S.-based human rights organization founded in 1988, which specializes in issues of fair trade and economic and social justice. Through educational and travel activities, they promote increased cross-cultural understanding and organizing.

Contact: kevin@global exchange.org
Web site: www.globalexchange.org

Greenpeace

Internationally chartered in 1978, the group engages in direct action. In campaigns, it is dedicated to providing information, applying political pressure, and researching energy alternatives. Currently operating in forty countries, the group has increased its work on North–South ecological questions.

Contact: supporter.services@int.greenpeace.org
Web site: www.greenpeace.org

HIC—Habitat International Coalition

HIC is an international movement that brings together four hundred organizations and individuals who work in the area of human settlements. Its objectives are the recognition and defense of a dignified and peaceful environment in which to live and the human right to housing.

Contact: hic-mena@hic-mena.org
Web site: www.hic-mena.org

IBASE—Brazilian Institute of Social and Economic Analyses

Founded in 1981 by Herbert de Souza, this is an institute directed at analysis and research about the Brazilian reality. Its objectives are to promote the demands of poor and excluded sectors, to develop actions that enable the imposition of public policies that prioritize equity and human development, to provide value and strengthen the citizenship participation of the poor, and to fight for the eradication of poverty.

Contact: imprensa@ibase.br
Web site: www.ibase.br

ICAE—International Council for Adult Education

Established in 1973, it is an association of adult learners, educators of adults, and organizations that promote the use of adult learning as a tool for sustainable development and citizen participation.

Contact: icae2@icae.org.uy
Web site: www.icae.org.uy

IFG—International Forum on Globalization

This is an alliance formed by activists, students, economists, researchers, and writers, working in twenty-five countries with the objective to stimulate new thinking, joint activity, and public education as a response to economic globalization.

Contact: ifg@ifg.org
Web site: www.ifg.org

IPS—Inter Press Service

Founded in 1964, this is an association of journalists and communications professionals that acts as a news agency and develops a system of intercultural communication. It promotes democratic participation in the social, political, and economic spheres; the full involvement of countries in the South in the definition of international policies; and empowerment of women in development.

Contact: headquarters@ips.org
Web site: www.ips.org

Jobs with Justice

Created in 1987 with the mission of improving the standard of living for workers, fighting for job security, and protecting workers' rights to form unions, it places the fight for workers' rights in the context of a community-wide campaign for social and economic justice.

Contact: info@jwj.org
Web site: www.jwj.org

Jubilee South

The group was formed by social movements on three continents of the South in Gauteng, South Africa, in November 1999;

more than 130 delegates from 35 countries were present, representing national and regional campaigns for canceling the debt. Its goals include debt cancellation, an end to structural adjustment, and the creation of a new world economic order that is people centered, sustainable, and democratic.

> Contact: secretariat@jubileesouth.org
> Web site: www.jubileesouth.org

KCTU—Korean Confederation of Trade Unions

Growing out of a federation of independent unions founded in 1990, it is the largest confederation of unions in Korea with industrial workers at its core.

> Contact: inter@kctu.org
> Web site: www.kctu.org

MST—Landless Rural Workers' Movement

Founded in 1984 during the First Conference of Landless Rural Workers, it organized nationally and promoted, in 1985, the First National Landless Congress. It works to construct a society without exploiters, in which work has supremacy over capital; to have the land as a common asset, at the service of the entire society; to guarantee work for all, with just distribution of land, income, and wealth; to seek social justice and equality of economic, political, social, and cultural rights; to spread humanist and socialist values in social relationships; to combat all forms of social discrimination; and to seek egalitarian participation of women.

> Contact: semterra@mst.org.br
> Web site: www.mst.org.br

NIGD—Network Institute for Global Democratization

A think tank founded in 1997 in Finland to promote democratization on the global level by means of production and development of emancipatory knowledge, it emphasizes dialogue between cultures, concerning both philosophical fundamentals and concrete reform proposals. Its projects are normally carried out with partners in the South.

Contact: nigd@nigd.org
Web site: www.nigd.org

North-South Centre

Established in 1989 by the European Council, it has the objective to encourage cooperation and solidarity between the North and South, aiming to improve education and information on global interdependence.

Contact: nscinfo@coe.int
Web site: www.coe.int/T/E/North-South_Centre

OCLAE—Continental Organization of Latin American and Caribbean Students

Arising from different student demonstrations at the beginning of the twentieth century, the organization promotes and develops solidarity among Latin American and Caribbean students, defends the autonomous university, and fights illiteracy and for free and public university education.

Contact: oclae@jcce.org.cu
Web site: www.oclae.org

ORIT—Regional Inter-American Organization of Workers

Founded in 1951 in Mexico, this organization brings together thirty-three confederations and central unions in twenty-nine countries in the Americas region. Its objectives include promoting the strengthening of autonomous, democratic, and ethical independent national labor unions that fight for political, social, and economic democracy.

> Contact: info@cioslorit.org
> Web site: www.cioslorit.org

OXFAM International

Chartered as an international organization in 1995, it has 1.5 million members. Twelve NGOs in rich countries that share the same objectives and work methods form the network. Its members work in eighty countries in the South jointly with three thousand popular organizations. Its areas of action are development projects, emergency assistance, fair trade, political pressure, research of development alternatives, education, and consciousness raising.

> Contact: information@oxfaminternational.org
> Web site: www.oxfam.org

Palestinian Non-Governmental Organizations' Network

A network of support, consolidation, and strengthening of Palestinian civil society, based on democracy, social justice, and sustainable development, it arose in 1993 when a group of Palestinian NGOs saw the necessity to reconsider the role and activities of NGOs in the political context of the region.

> Contact: pngonet@pngo.net (West Bank)
> Web site: www.pngo.net

PIDHDD—Inter-American Platform of Human Rights, Democracy, and Development

Founded in 1992 in Colombia, this is a plural, convergent,

and autonomous association of diverse civil society organizations in Latin America and the Caribbean. It seeks to promote information exchange, formation and elaboration of demandable and verifiable human rights proposals, as well as economic, social, and cultural rights.

Contact: regional@pidhdd.org
Web site: www.pidhdd.org

Public Citizen

Founded in 1971 by Ralph Nader, this is a North American organization whose objectives are to represent the interests of consumers in Congress, the executive branch, and the courts. It fights for open and transparent government; for consumers' rights; for clean, secure, and sustainable energy sources; for social and economic justice in trade policies, health, and the environment; and for accessible medications and health services.

Contact: member@citizen.org
Web site: www.citizen.org

Social Network for Justice and Human Rights

Created in 2002, this network formulates petitions and solicits for cases to national and international organizations, participates in emergency delegations in conflict areas and situations, observes trials, operates campaigns against impunity, holds trainings on juridical mechanisms for human rights defense, and promotes publications and media interventions.

Contact: rede@social.org.br
Web site: www.social.org.br

Social Watch

Founded in 1995, this is the fruit of civil society forums held parallel to UN summits on world development and women. The network, whose coordination is the job of the Third World Institute of Montevideo, monitors the policies for compliance with the agreements signed in the two summits. Each year it evaluates the public policies of governments, publishes the newsletter "Citizen Control," and makes proposals to advance social development in the South.

Contact: socwatch@socialwatch.org
Web site: www.socialwatch.org

Solidar

An independent alliance of NGOs involved in social cooperation, international cooperative work, and humanitarian assistance, it was established in Germany in 1951 under the name International Workers Aid. It moved to Brussels in 1995 and was renamed Solidar.

Contact: solidar@skynet.be
Web site: www.solidar.org

TNI—Transnational Institute

Founded in 1974 as the first transnational institute in name, composition, orientation, and focus, it promotes international cooperation and seeks possible solutions to global problems such as militarism and conflicts, marginalization and poverty, social injustice, and environmental degradation.

Contact: tni@tni.org
Web site: www.tni.org

TWN—Third World Network

Founded in 1984 in Penang, Malaysia, it also has headquarters in Ghana and Uruguay. Its objectives are to investigate the social problems of poor countries, propose action plans, work to influence governments in the South, and publish newsletters, documents, books, etc. Social Watch coordinates its Latin American network. In recent years, it has focused its work on the WTO and the environment.

Contact: twnet@po.jaring.my
Web site: www.twnside.org.sg

Via Campesina

The Landless Movement and the Peasants' Federation in France were the main founders of this group, which was created in 1993. Organizations of small- and medium-scale farmers, landless agricultural workers' unions, associations of rural women, and indigenous people constitute it. The network's international work is based on several points: ecological agriculture, rural women and indigenous people, agrarian reform, food sovereignty, biodiversity, biosecurity, and genetic resources.

Contact: viacampesina@multivisionhn.net
Web site: www.viacampesina.org

WCL—World Confederation of Labor

Created in 1920 under the name International Confederation of Christian Unions, it inspires the values of Christian humanism. In recent years, the WCL has adopted a posture critical of neoliberalism. It defends social development that goes beyond respect for workers and the elimination of poverty, as well as the regulatory role of the state and equal distribution of the goods and means of production.

Contact: info@cmt-wcl.org
Web site: www.cmt-wcl.org

WFA—World Forum for Alternatives

Created in 1997 in Lovaine, Belgium, this forum groups the organizations of CETRI (Belgium), Third World Forum (Senegal), FUNDE (El Salvador), Focus on the Global South (Thailand), Alternatives (Canada), CEDETIM (France), and Punto Rosso (Italy). The network has as its objectives considering alternatives to globalization in a postcapitalist perspective and conducting an analytical inventory of social movements in the South. It publishes the magazine *Alternatives Sud* and the annual report "Globalization of Resistance: The State of Struggles."

Contact: info@social-movements.org
Web site: www.social-movements.org

World March of Women

Born in 1995 in a forum held during the Beijing Summit, it was driven by the Quebec Women's Federation and is made up currently of 5,500 women's movements in 163 countries. It organizes marches against issues such as poverty and violence. The first march was held in Canada, and from 1995 to 2000 nationally and internationally coordinated marches were organized, ending in a rally at the United Nations headquarters in New York.

Contact: info@marchemondiale.org
Web site: http://www.marchemondiale.org

Chronology

1997

January: Beginning of dissemination of first drafts of the Multilateral Agreement on Investment (MAI)

April 14–June 14: First European rally against unemployment, exclusion, and insecurity, ending in Amsterdam, Holland, with approximately fifty thousand people

May 15: Formation of the Continental Social Alliance (CSA) in the meeting of the Third Trade Union Summit, held parallel to the ministerial meeting of the FTAA in Belo Horizonte, Brazil

June 26–August 3: Intercontinental Meeting for Humanity and Against Neoliberalism in Barcelona, Spain; the proposal for Peoples' Global Action is presented; the group is officially formed in February 1998

September: Asian financial crisis explodes

Decade of the 1980s
Initiation of the implementation of neoliberal policies by the governments of Margaret Thatcher (United Kingdom) and Ronald Reagan (United States)

November 1989
Fall of the Berlin Wall

1991
End of the USSR and the formation of the Commonwealth of Independent States

1991–92
Disintegration of Yugoslavia; Balkans War

January–February 1991
First Gulf War against Iraq

January 1994
Popular uprising organized by the Zapatista Army for National Liberation in Chiapas, Mexico

1994
Genocide in Rwanda leaves 500,000 dead

July 27–August 3, 1996
First Intercontinental Meeting for Humanity and Against Neoliberalism in Chiapas, Mexico

October: Formation of Jubilee 2000, constituted by Christian and social organizations that demand the cancellation of the external debt

1998

February 12: Coordinated campaign launched against the MAI at the same time that the Organization for Economic Co-operation and Development (OECD) officially publicizes the proposal

April 15–18: People's Summit of the Americas, held parallel to the Presidential Summit of the Americas, under the umbrella of activities of the CSA

April 27: Protest against the OECD, which will deal with negotiations of the MAI in Paris; from this point on, the OECD decides the approval of the MAI

May 16–18: Protests and mobilizations against the annual meeting of the G-8 in Birmingham, England, and the Second Ministerial Meeting of the WTO in Geneva, Switzerland

June 29–30: First meeting of the Coordinator of the Central Trade Unions of the Southern Cone (CCSCS) and the Andean Consultative Labor Council

July 3: Formation of ATTAC in Paris

October: Protests against the MAI throughout the month in different countries; the OECD terminates the agreement, suspending negotiations

1999

January 27-31: The international meeting "Another Davos" in Zurich, Switzerland, simultaneous to the meeting of the World Economic Forum

March-June: NATO war in Kosovo

June 18: Protests in various financial centers around the world

June 24-26: International meeting "Another World Is Possible" in Paris, organized by ATTAC, CADTM, and the World Alternatives Forum, among others

October 12: First Latin American Cry of the Excluded using the slogan, "For Work, Justice, and Life"

November 18-21: International meeting for Abolition of Third World Debt and the South-South Summit about the debt in Johannesburg, South Africa

November 30: Thousands of people protest in Seattle against the WTO Millennium Round, disrupting the negotiations on the second day of the summit

2000

January 21: Popular and indigenous uprising in Ecuador

January 29: Protests in opposition to the World Economic Forum in Davos, Switzerland

February 12: Protests and mobilizations in Bangkok, Thailand, against the tenth United Nations Conference on Trade and Development (UNCTAD) Summit

March 8: Beginning of the World March of Women 2000; different activities promoted through October 17, when a march ended with a mobilization in front of the United Nations

April 16: Protests and mobilizations in Washington, D.C., in opposition to the International Monetary Fund meeting

May 1: Mobilizations throughout the world on International Labor Day, considered the fourth Day of Global Action

May 6–8: Thousands of activists protest in Chiang Mai, Thailand, in opposition to the annual meeting of the Asian Development Bank (ADB)

June 4: Protests in Windsor, Canada, against the meeting of the Organization of American States

June 12–15: Demonstration of the Tute Bianche in Bologna, Italy, against the OECD meeting

June 22–25: Alternative Summit to the Second Social Development Summit organized by the United Nations in Geneva, Switzerland

June 30–July 1: Thirty thousand people mobilize in protest against the trial of José Bové and the other militants of the peasants confederation in Millau, France, and an international meeting against financial globalization is held

June 21–23: Demonstrations demanding abolition of Third World debt and the removal of North American military bases from Japan are held in Okinawa, Japan, during the G-7 meeting

July 31–August 3: Around twenty thousand people protest during the Republican National Convention in Philadelphia, demanding the right to abortion and an end to the death penalty, police brutality, environmental destruction, and the U.S. military occupation of the island of Vieques, Puerto Rico; activists from the National Organization for Women (NOW) and the Black Bloc participate

August 30: Second meeting of the CCSCS and the Andean Consultative Labor Council simultaneous to the Meeting of Heads of State of South America in Brasilia, Brazil ("the Brasilia Summit")

September 6: Third International Conference of Via Campesina in Bangalore, India

September 8: Protests during the Millennium Meeting of the United Nations

September 11–13: Protests in Melbourne, Australia, against the World Economic Forum; some delegations are prevented from entering the headquarters, which are encircled by thirty thousand demonstrators

September 26: Fifth Day of Global Action on the occasion of the annual meeting of the IMF and World Bank in Prague, Czech Republic; more than fifteen thousand people participate in the protests, which caused the meeting to end early; demonstrations held in more than forty countries

October 14–17: Culmination of the World March of Women

December 5-6: Mobilizations and protests in Nice, France, against the European Union Summit

December 12-17: International Meeting of Dakar 2000, "From Resistances to Alternatives," with aims of annulling the debt and abandoning structural adjustment programs in the Third World

2001

January 25-30: First World Social Forum in Porto Alegre, Brazil

February 26-27: Protests organized by F26, CSA, and the Coordination of Civil Disobedience, among other organizations

March 15-17: More than forty thousand people demonstrate in Naples, Italy, against the Third Global Forum Fostering Democracy and Development through E-Government

April 5-6: More than twelve thousand demonstrators protest in Buenos Aires against the FTAA meeting

April 20-22: Thousands demonstrate in Quebec, Canada, against the Summit of the Americas (a meeting of presidents of the Americas) and are strongly repressed; a Second People's Summit is held

June 22-25: The Barcelona Social Forum is held concurrent to the World Bank meeting, which was canceled

June 13-17: More than twenty thousand activists protest on the occasion of the meeting of Chiefs of State of the European Union and the visit of President George W. Bush to the summit in Göteborg, Sweden

July 18-21: Three days of protest against the G-8 meeting in Genoa, Italy; demonstrators are violently repressed and one, Carlo Giuliani, is killed by Italian police

August 31-September 7: UN World Conference Against Racism, Racial Discrimination, Xenophobia, and Related Intolerance in Durban, South Africa

September 11: Terrorist attacks against the World Trade Center and Pentagon

November 9-14: Fourth Ministerial Meeting of the WTO in Doha, Qatar; the conference location makes demonstrations difficult

December 14-15: Around twenty-five thousand people protest during the Laeken European Summit in Brussels, Belgium; the European Confederation of Labor Unions, ATTAC, and the network D14, among others, participate in organizing the demonstrations

December 19-20: The Argentinazo: mass demonstrations break the Argentine government's attempt to enforce a state of siege against food riots; neoliberal De La Rua government is forced from office

2002

January 25-27: First Pan-Amazon Forum in Belém, Brazil

January 31-February 5: Second World Social Forum in Porto Alegre, Brazil

February 2002: Protests in New York against the World Economic Forum of Davos and the IMF

March 15-16: Demonstrations, workshops, and seminars, organized by the Campaign against a Europe of Capitalism and War, in Barcelona, Spain, on the occasion of the European Union Summit

March 18-22: Global Forum in Monterrey, Mexico, in opposition to the United Nations International Conference on Financing for Development

April 19-22: Meeting and demonstration in Washington, D.C., of the movements against capitalist globalization, against the war, and for solidarity with Palestine, together with movements against cutting state expenditures and the loss of civil liberties; on April 20, a huge march of about 200,000

May 17-18: Demonstrations in Madrid, on the occasion of the Second Summit of the European Union, Latin America, and the Caribbean; from May 13–19, the Transatlantic Social Forum

June 21-22: The Seville Social Forum in opposition to the meeting of the European Union Summit in Seville, Spain

August 22-25: The Argentina Thematic Social Forum in Buenos Aires, Argentina

October 27-November 1: The Campaign against the FTAA and Continental Days of Resistance Rally in Quito, Ecuador

November 6-10: First European Social Forum in Florence, Italy

December 27-30: Palestine Thematic Social Forum in Ramallah, Palestine

2003

January 2-7: Asian Social Forum in Hyderabad, India

January 5-9: Second African Social Forum in Addis Ababa, Ethiopia

January 16-19: Second Pan-Amazon Social Forum in Belém, Brazil

January 23-28: Third World Social Forum in Porto Alegre, Brazil

February 15: International demonstration against the impending war in Iraq; as many as ten million participate worldwide

March 20: The United States launches attacks against Iraq

June 16-20: Thematic Social Forum For Democracy and Human Rights and Against War and Narcotrafficking, Cartagena de las Indias, Colombia

September 10-15: Protests force collapse of World Trade Organization ministerial meeting, Cancún, México

October 15- 17: Mass demonstrations, beginning as protests over the privatization and export of Bolivian natural gas, bring down the Bolivian government

November 12-15: European Social Forum in Paris/St. Denis, France

2004

January 16-21: About 75,000 participants from 117 countries attend fourth World Social Forum held in Mumbai, India

February 4-8: Pan-Amazon Social Forum held in Ciudad Guayana, Venezuela

July 23-25: Five thousand attend Boston Social Forum, the largest social forum held to date in North America

July 25-30: First Social Forum of the Americas held in Quito, Ecuador. More than 20,000 participate in forum

August 31: More than 500,000 march in New York against the "Bush agenda" at the Republican National Convention

October 15-17: European Social Forum held in London. More than 20,000 from 70 countries attend.

November 19-21: First Social Forum in Chile mobilizes more than 50,000 to protest the Asian-Pacific Economic Cooperation meeting and the presence of U.S. President George W. Bush

2005

January 18-22: Pan-Amazon Social Forum, held in Manaus, Amazonas, Brazil

January 26-31: Fifth World Social Forum, held in Porto Alegre, Brazil

June 16-19: Mediterranean Social Forum, held in Barcelona, Spain

Selected Bibliography

A GENERAL COMMENT

Most of the pertinent texts about the World Social Forum are available on the Internet, principally at the forum's Web site, http://forumsocialmundial.org.br. Other sites offer access to vast material about the global movement (see the following).

The bibliography is organized by chapters, but it is worthwhile to highlight some titles.

In the first chapter, *The Age of Extremes,* by Eric Hobsbawm, continues to be the best overview of the political twentieth century and the impact of its abrupt termination in 1989–91. David Harvey, Frederic Jameson, François Chesnais, and Peter Gowan offer important analytical references to comprehend the changes over the past twenty years (also debated by analysts of the system, such as Paul Krugman and Joseph Stiglitz).

Immanuel Wallerstein and Pierre Bourdieu already participated in this debate, anticipating orientations and controversies of the movement that have developed since Seattle—which also recall the work of Guy Debord. It is important to read the Zapatista texts in *A revolução invencível* (Invincible Revolution), which offer a basis for the theorizing of John Holloway. Ignacio Ramonet and Susan George initiated the movement in France in the 1990s, and their texts are emblematic. Claude Sefarti, Eric Toussaint, Ricardo Petrella, and Vandana Shiva have already worked for many years on the themes of militarization, the debt, and common assets.

In the second chapter, Christophe Aguiton gives the best overview of the movement's formation in his book *The World Belongs to Us,* but the works of Walden Bello, François Houtart, and Naomi Klein express central positions of the global movement. The book by José Bové, *O mundo não é uma mercadoria* (The World Is Not a Product), deals in one of its central aspects with the struggle of farmworkers and the formation of Via Campesina.

About the first World Social Forum, the best book is the one edited by José Seoane and Emilio Taddei, *Resistências mundiales* (Worldwide Resistances). The documents and reports of the International Council and the WSF Organizing Committee, as well as the individual analyses and evaluations of its members, can be read at the forum site. An enormous number of informative articles and analyses can be found in magazines and in the other Web sites listed at the end of this bibliography.

The bibliography of the fourth chapter deals with very distinct themes: the change in the political reality post–September 11, 2001; the second and third World Social Forums (including the proposals and alternatives presented in them); and the theoretical debates that have been distilling in recent years. *O espírito de Porto Alegre* (The Spirit of Porto Alegre) groups texts that attempt to articulate these different aspects. *The Algebra of Infinite Justice* by Arundhati Roy, perhaps the most brilliant essayist of the movement, is available only in English and Spanish. About the new international situation, the following authors should be noted: Gilbert Achcar, Tariq Ali, Noam Chomsky, Ana Esther Ceceña, and Emir Sader. About the forum process and its proposals, the best work is that edited by William F. Fisher and Thomas Ponniah about the second WSF, but the book by Rafael Díaz-Salazar is also very useful. Authors such as Antonio Negri, Holloway, and Klein propose new issues for the global movement from a perspective that we could, schematically, consider as part of the libertarian current. Wallerstein, Bello, Daniel Bensaïd, and Atílio Boron intervene in the strategic debate, rescuing conceptions that can be considered closer to the Marxist tradition, even if in some cases very redefined.

Introduction and Chapter I

AMIN, Samir. *Capitalism in the Age of Globalization: The Management of Contemporary Society*. London: Zed Books, 1997.

ARANTES, Paulo. *Notícias de uma guerra cosmopolita*. Mimeo, 2003.

ARRIGHI, Giovanni. *The Long Twentieth Century: Money, Power, and the Origins of Our Times*. London and New York: Verso, 1994.

―――――. *A ilusão do desenvolvimento*. Petrópolis: Vozes, 1998.

BATISTA JR., Paulo Nogueira. "Mitos da 'globalização'". *Estudos Avançados* 12, no. 32 (January–April 1998): 125–86.

BELLO, Walden, Nicola Bullard, and Kamal Malhotra, eds. *Global Finance: New Thinking on Regulating Speculative Capital Markets*. London: Zed Books, 2000.

BENSAÏD, Daniel. *Contes et légendes de la guerre éthique*. Paris: Textuel, 1999.

―――――. *Le nouvel internationalisme contre les guerres impériales et la privatisation du monde*. Paris: Textuel, 2003.

BOURDIEU, Pierre. *Contre-feux: Propos pour servir à la résistance contre l'invasion néo-libérale*. Paris: Editions Liber, 1998.

―――――. *Contre-feux 2: Pour un mouvement social européen*. Paris : Raisons d'agir, 2001.

CHESNAIS, François. *A mundialização do capital*. São Paulo: Xamã, 1996.

CANCLINI, Néstor García. *La globalización imaginada*. Buenos Aires: Paidós, 1999.

CHANDRASEKHAR, C. P. and Jayati Ghosh. *The Market That Failed: A Decade of Neoliberal Economic Reforms in India*. New Delhi: Leftword, 2002.

COUTROUT, Thomas and Michel Husson. *Les destins du Tiers Monde*. Paris: Nathan, 1993.

DEBORD, Guy. *The Society of the Spectacle*. New York: Zone Books, 1994.

DI FELICE, Massimo and Cristobal Muñoz, eds. *A revolução invencível: Subcomandante Marcos e Exército Zapatista de Libertação Nacional: cartas e comunicados*. São Paulo: Boitempo, 1998.

DOWBOR, Ladislau, Octavio Ianni, and Paulo-Edgar A. Resende, eds. *Desafios da globalização*. Petrópolis: Vozes, 1999.

DUSSEL, Enrique. *Ética da libertação na idade da globalização e da exclusão*. Petrópolis: Vozes, 2000.

FONTENELLE, Isleide Arruda. *O nome da marca: McDonald's, fetichismo e cultura descartável*. São Paulo: Fapesp/Boitempo, 2002.

FORRESTER, Viviane. *The Economic Horror*. Translated from French. Cambridge, UK: Polity Press; Oxford, UK, and Malden, MA: Blackwell, 1999.

FUKUYAMA, Francis. *The End of History and the Last Man*. New York: Free Press; Toronto: Maxwell Macmillan Canada; New York: Maxwell Macmillan International, 1992.

FIORI, José Luis and Carlos Medeiros, eds. *Polarização mundial e crescimento*. Petrópolis: Vozes, 2001.

GEORGE, Susan. *The Lugano Report: On Preserving Capitalism in the Twenty-First Century*. London and Sterling, Virginia: Pluto Press, 2003.

——— and Fabrizio Sabelli. *Faith and Credit: The World Bank's Secular Empire*. Boulder: Westview Press, 1994.

GOWAN, Peter. *The Global Gamble: Washington's Faustian Bid for World Dominance*. London and New York: Verso, 1999.

HARVEY, David. *The Condition of Postmodernity: An Enquiry into the Origins of Cultural Change.* Oxford, UK, and Cambridge, Massachusetts: Blackwell, 1989.

HIRST, Paul and Grahame Thompson. *Globalization in Question: The International Economy and the Possibilities of Governance.* 2nd ed. Cambridge, UK, and Malden, Massachusetts: Polity, 1999.

HOBSBAWM, Eric. *Age of Extremes: The Short Twentieth Century, 1914–1991.* New York: First Vintage Books Edition, 1996.

HUSSON, Michel. *Le grand bluff capitaliste.* Paris: La Dispute, 2001.

——— et al. *Mondialisation et impérialisme.* Paris: Syllepse, 2003.

JAMESON, Fredric. *Postmodernism, or, The Cultural Logic of Late Capitalism.* Durham, North Carolina: Duke University Press, 1991.

———. *A cultura do dinheiro: Ensaios sobre a globalização.* Petrópolis: Vozes, 2001.

JAPPE, Anselm. *Guy Debord.* Donald Nicholson-Smith, trans. Berkeley, California: University of California Press, 1999.

KRUGMAN, Paul. *Pop Internationalism.* Cambridge, Massachusetts: MIT Press, 1996.

LASCH, Christophe. *The Minimal Self: Psychic Survival in Troubled Times.* 1st ed. New York: W.W. Norton, 1984.

———. *The Revolt of the Elites and the Betrayal of Democracy.* 1st ed. New York: W.W. Norton, 1995.

LÖWY, Michael and Daniel Bensaïd. *Marxismo, modernidade e*

utopia. São Paulo: Xamã, 2000.

MANDEL, Ernst. *Late Capitalism*. Joris De Bres, trans. Revised ed. Atlantic Highlands, New Jersey: Humanities Press, 1975.

MCCHESNEY, Robert, Ellen Meiksins Wood, and John Bellamy Foster. *Capitalism and the Information Age: The Political Economy of the Global Communication Revolution*. New York: Monthly Review Press, 1998.

OHMAE, Kenichi. *The End of the Nation State: The Rise of Regional Economies*. New York: Free Press, 1995.

PASSET, René. *L'économique et le vivant*. Paris, Econômica, 1996.

PETRELLA, Ricardo. *The Water Manifesto: Arguments for a World Water Contract*. Patrick Camiller, trans. London and New York: Zed Books, 2001.

RAMONET, Ignacio. *Geopolitics of Chaos*. Andrea Lyn Secara, trans. New York: Algora, 1998.

———. *A tirania da comunicação*. Petrópolis, Vozes, 1999.

RIFKIN, Jeremy. *The End of Work: The Decline of the Global Labor Force and the Dawn of the Post-Market Era*. New York: G.P. Putnam's Sons, 1995.

ROUDINESCO, Elisabeth. *Why Psychoanalysis?* Rachel Bowlby, trans. New York: Columbia University Press, 2001.

SANTOS, Milton. *Por uma outra globalização*. Rio de Janeiro: Record, 2000.

SERFATI, Claude. *La mondialisation armée: Le déséquilibre de la terreur*. Paris: Textuel, 2001.

SHIVA, Vandana. *Biopiracy: The Plunder of Nature and Knowl-*

edge. Boston: South End Press, 1997.

SOARES, Laura Tavares Ribeiro. *Ajuste neoliberal e desajuste social na América Latina*. Petrópolis: Vozes/LPP/CLACSO, 2001.

STIGLITZ, Joseph. *Globalization and Its Discontents*. New York: W.W. Norton, 2003.

TAVARES, Maria da Conceição and José Luis Fiori, eds. *Poder e dinheiro: uma economia poítica da globalização*. 3rd ed. Petrópolis: Vozes, 1997.

TOUSSAINT, ERIC. *Your Money or Your Life!: The Tyranny of Global Finance*. Raghu Krishnan, trans., with the collaboration of Vicki Briault Manus. London and Sterling, Virginia: Pluto Press, 1999. New edition forthcoming, spring 2005, from Haymarket Books.

VIEIRA, Liszt. *Os argonautas da cidadania: a sociedade civil na globalização*. Rio de Janeiro: Record, 2001.

WALLERSTEIN, Immanuel. *After Liberalism*. New York: New Press, 1995.

WENT, Robert. *Globalization: Neoliberal Challenge, Radical Responses*. Peter Drucker, trans. London and Sterling, Virginia: Pluto Press/IIRE, 2000.

WOOD, Ellen Meiksins. *Democracy against Capitalism: Renewing Historical Materialism*. Cambridge and New York: Cambridge University Press, 1995.

Chapter II

AGUITON, Christophe. *Le monde nous appartient*. Paris: Plon, 2001.

AMAT, Dolores, Pedro Brieger, Luciana Ghiotto, Maité Llanos, and Mariana Percovich. "La globalización neoliberal y las nuevas redes de resistencia global." *Cuaderno de Trabajo,* no. 8 (November 2002). Buenos Aires: Centro Cultural de la Cooperación.

BELLO, Walden. *The Future in the Balance: Essays on Globalization and Resistance.* Oakland, California: Food First Books, 2001.

BOND, Patrick. *Against Global Apartheid: South Africa Meets the World Bank, IMF, and International Finance.* New York: Zed Books, 2003.

BOVÉ, José and François Dufour. *The World Is Not for Sale: Farmers against Junk Food.* Interviewed by Gilles Luneau. Anna de Casparis, trans. London and New York: Verso, 2001.

CHRISPINIANO, José. *A guerrilha surreal.* São Paulo: Conrad/Com-Arte, 2002.

CRITICAL ART ENSEMBLE. *Distúrbio eletrônico.* São Paulo: Conrad, 2001.

DANAHER, Kevin and Roger Burbach, eds. *Globalize This!: The Battle against the World Trade Organization and Corporate Rule.* Monroe, Maine: Common Courage Press, 2000.

GEORGE, Susan. "Comment l'OMC fut mise en échec." *Le Monde Diplomatique* (January 2000): 4–5.

HOUTART, François. *La tiranía del mercado y sus alternativas.* Madrid: Editorial Popular, 2001.

——— and François Polet, eds. *The Other Davos Summit: The Globalization of Resistance to the World Economic Sys-*

tem. London and New York: Zed Books, 2001.

INTERNACIONAL SITUACIONISTA. *Situacionista: Teoria e prática da revolução*. São Paulo: Conrad, 2002.

KLEIN, Naomi. *No Logo: Taking Aim at the Brand Bullies*. New York: Picador, 2000.

MONTESINOS, Miguel Riera, ed. *La batalla de Génova*. Barcelona: El Viejo Topo, 2001.

MUNCK, Ronaldo. *Globalisation and Labour: The New "Great Transformation."* London: Zed Books, 2002.

PASTOR, Jaime. *Qué son los movimientos antiglobalización*. Barcelona: RBA Libros, 2002.

ROMA, Pepa. *Jaque a la globalización: Como crean su red los nuevos movimientos sociales y alternativos*. Barcelona: Mondadori, 2002.

ST. CLAIR, Jeffrey. "Seattle Diary: It's a Gas, Gas, Gas!" *CounterPunch,* December 16, 1999. http://www.counterpunch.org/seattlediary.html.

TABB, William K. *The Amoral Elephant: Globalization and the Struggle for Social Justice in the Twenty-first Century*. New York: Monthly Review Press, 2001.

ZIZEK, Slavoj. *Le spectre rôde toujours*. Paris: Nautilus, 2002.

Chapter III

AMIN, Samir et al. *Otro mundo es posible: Foro Social Mundial—Porto Alegre, 2001*. Buenos Aires: Desde la gente, 2001.

ASSUNÇÃO, Jefferson and Zaira Machado. *O mundo das alternativas: Pequeno dicionário para uma globalização soli-*

dária. Porto Alegre: Veraz, 2001.

GENRO, Tarso et al. *Por uma nova esfera pública: A experiência do orçamento participativo.* Petrópolis: Vozes, 2000.

PONT, Raul. *Democracia, participação e cidadania: Uma visão de esquerda.* Porto Alegre: Palmarinca, 2000.

——— and Adair Barcelos, eds. *Porto Alegre uma cidade que conquista: A terceira gestão do PT na governo municipal.* Porto Alegre: Artes e Ofícios, 2000.

SEOANE, José and Emilio Taddei, eds. *Resistencias mundiales: De Seattle a Porto Alegre.* Buenos Aires: Consejo Latinoamericano de Ciencias Sociales, 2001.

WHITAKER, Francisco. "Fórum Social Mundial: Origem e objetivos." Originally published in *Correio da Cidadania,* and available on the World Social Forum Web site, www.forumsocialmundial.org.br.

Chapter IV

ACHCAR, Gilbert. *The Clash of Barbarisms: September 11 and the Making of the New World Disorder.* New York: Monthly Review Press, 2002.

ALI, Tariq. *The Clash of Fundamentalisms: Crusades, Jihads and Modernity.* London: Verso, 2002.

BARSAMIAN, David and Noam Chomsky. *Propaganda and the Public Mind: Conversations with Noam Chomsky.* Cambridge, Massachusetts: South End Press, 2001.

BELLO, Walden. *Deglobalization: Ideas for a New World Economy.* London and New York: Zed Books, 2004.

BENSAÏD, Daniel. *Un monde à changer: Mouvements et straté-*

gies. Paris: Textuel, 2003.

———. *Le nouvel internationalisme contre les guerres impériales et la privatisation du monde.* Paris: Textuel, 2003.

———. *Résistances: Essai de taupologie générale.* Paris: Fayard, 2001.

BORÓN, Atilio. *Imperio & imperialismo: Una lectura crítica de Michael Hardt y Antonio Negri.* Buenos Aires: CLACSO–Consejo Latinoamericano de Ciencias Sociales, Secretaría Ejecutiva, 2002.

CECEÑA, Ana Esther and Emir Sader, eds. *La guerra infinita: Hegemonía y terror mundial.* Buenos Aires: CLACSO–Consejo Latinoamericano de Ciencias Sociales, 2002.

CHANDLER, David. *From Kosovo to Kabul: Human Rights and International Intervention.* London and Sterling, Virginia: Pluto Press, 2002.

CHEMILLIER-GENDREAU, Monique. *Droit international et démocratie mondiale: Les raisons d'un échec.* Paris: Textuel, 2002.

CHESNAIS, François. *Tobin or not Tobin?: Por que tributar o capital financeiro internacional em apoio aos cidadãos.* São Paulo: Edunesp, 1999.

CHOMSKY, Noam. *9-11.* New York: Seven Stories Press, 2002.

COCCO, Giuseppe and Graziela Hopstein. *As multidões e o império.* Rio de Janeiro: DP&A, 2002.

DÍAZ-SALAZAR, Rafael, ed. *Justicia global: Las alternativas de los movimientos del Foro de Porto Alegre.* Barcelona: Icaria-Intermón Oxfam, 2002.

FISHER, William F. and Thomas Ponniah, eds. *Another World Is Possible: Popular Alternatives to Globalization at the World Social Forum.* New York and London: Zed Books, 2003.

GRUPO KRISIS. *Manifesto contra o trabalho.* São Paulo: Geousp Labur, 1999.

HARDT, Michael and Antonio Negri. *Empire.* Cambridge, Massachusetts: Harvard University Press, 2000.

HOLLOWAY, John. *Change the World without Taking Power.* London and Sterling, Virginia: Pluto Press, 2002.

ISAAC, T. M. Thomas and Richard Franke. *Local Democracy and Development: The Kerala People's Campaign for Decentralized Planning.* New Delhi: LeftWord, 2000.

JETIN, Bruno. *La taxe Tobin et la solidarité entre les nations.* Paris: Descartes et Cie, 2002.

LOUÇÃ, Francisco and Jorge Costa. *A guerra infinita.* Lisbon: Afrontamento, 2003.

LOUREIRO, Isabel, José Correa Leite, and Maria Elisa Cevasco, eds. *O espírito de Porto Alegre.* São Paulo: Paz e Terra, 2002.

MADELEY, John. *O comércio da fome.* Petrópolis: Vozes, 2003.

NEGRI, Toni et al. *Contrapoder, una introducción.* Buenos Aires: De mano en mano, 2001.

PATOMÄKI, Heikki, Teivo Teivainen, and Mika Rönkkö. *Global Democracy Initiatives: The Art of Possible.* Helsinki: NIGD, 2002.

PRASHAD, Vijay. *War Against the Planet: The Fifth Afghan War, Imperialism, and Other Assorted Fundamentalisms.* New Delhi: LeftWord, 2002.

PURKAYASTHA, Prabir and Vijay Prashad. *Enron Blowout: Corporate Capitalism and Theft of the Global Commons.* New Delhi: LeftWord, 2002.

RIKKILÄ, Leena and Katarina Sehm Patomäki, eds. *From a Global Market Place to Political Spaces: The North-South Dialogue Continues.* Nottingham and Helsinki: NIGD, 2002.

ROY, Arundhati. *The Algebra of Infinite Justice.* New Delhi: Penguin Books, 2002.

SADER, Emir. *A vingança da história.* São Paulo: Boitempo, 2003.

TODD, Emmanuel. *After the Empire: The Breakdown of the American Order.* C. Jon Delogu, trans. New York: Columbia University Press, 2003.

VARIOUS AUTHORS. *Porto Alegre, Foro Social Mundial, 2002: una asamblea de la humanidad.* 1st ed. Barcelona: Icaria; Montevideo, Uruguay: Instituto del Tercer Mundo, 2002.

WOOD, Ellen Meiksins. *Empire of Capital.* London and New York: Verso, 2003.

ZIZEK, Slavoj. *Revolution at the Gates.* London, Verso, 2004.

———. *The Ticklish Subject: The Absent Centre of Political Ontology.* London and New York: Verso, 1999.

MAGAZINES

Actuel Marx (Paris).

Contretemps (Paris).

Erre (Rome).

Le Monde Diplomatique (Paris).

Mientras Tanto (Barcelona).

Monthly Review (New York).

New Left Review (London).

Observatorio Social de América Latina (Buenos Aires)

Viento Sur (Madrid).

WEB SITES

ATTAC—www.attac.org

CADTM (Committee for the Abolition of the Third World Debt)—www.cadtm.org

Common Dreams—www.commondreams.org

CounterPunch—www.counterpunch.org

Focus on the Global South—www.focusweb.org

Independent Media Center—www.indymedia.org

Porto Alegre 2003—www.portoalegre2003.org

Rebelión—www.rebelion.org

World Social Forum (Fórum Social Mundial)—www.forumsocialmundial.org.br

ZNet—www.zmag.org

Index

A

Addis Ababa, (Ethiopia) 128, 240
Afghanistan, 18, 103, 110, 120, 152, 159, 188, 197, 206
AFL-CIO (American Federation of Labor—Congress of Industrial Organizations), 45, 57, 62, 66, 170, 210
African Social Forum, 125, 128, 240
Agnoletto, Victorio, 97
Aguiton, Christophe, 167, 171, 242
Amin, Samir, 36
Anti-Capitalist Youth, 175
Arrighi, Giovanni, 28
Asian Social Forum, 120, 128–30, 146, 155, 240
ATTAC (Association for the Taxation of Financial Transactions for the Aid of Citizens), 51–52, 67, 74, 78, 80–84, 86, 97, 113, 167, 170, 212, 233–34, 238, 255

B

Bangkok (Thailand), 65, 79, 116, 234
Bangladesh, 129, 152, 219
Barcelona (Spain), 51, 104, 116, 124, 125, 132, 136, 194, 232, 237, 239
Barcelona Social Forum, 69, 237
Barlow, Maude, 60
Basque Country, 108
Batista, Paulo Nogueira, Jr., 21
Belgium, 42, 135, 158, 213, 229, 238
Bello, Walden, 50, 60, 64, 177, 242, 243
Bensaïd, Daniel, 25, 31, 243
Berlin Wall, 15, 24, 70, 231
Berlusconi, Silvio, 69, 72, 126
Betto, Frei, 87
Bharatiya Janata Party (BJP), 150
Bissio, Roberto, 97
Boeing, 46, 177
Boff, Leonardo, 87
Bourdieu, Pierre, 50, 241

Bové, José, 61, 66, 87, 89, 169, 235, 242
Brazil, 24–25, 39, 47, 50–51, 68, 78, 91, 95, 104, 122, 130, 135–36, 145, 161, 165, 169–71, 202, 210, 213, 215–16, 232, 236–40
Brazilian Organizing Committee, 13, 80, 82, 95-99, 111–116, 119, 123, 132, 162
Bretton Woods, 26, 71
Brussels (Belgium), 65, 135, 227, 238
Buenos Aires (Argentina), 48, 62, 68–69, 91, 125, 186, 195, 214, 237, 239
Bullard, Nicola, 97, 175
Bush, George H.W., 41
Bush, George W., 17, 69, 70, 72, 92, 104, 134, 138, 142, 152, 153, 170, 177, 237

C

CADTM (Committee for the Abolition of Third World Debt), 97, 113, 213, 234, 255
Canada, 32–33, 42, 68–69, 186, 195, 215, 229, 235, 237
Canclini, Néstor García, 37
Cancún (Mexico), 160, 207
Caracas (Venezuela), 136
Cassen, Bernard, 78–79, 97, 167
Caterpillar, 177
Cavanagh, John, 60
Charter of Principles, WSF, 9–13, 97, 99, 100–102, 109, 111, 132, 139–40, 146, 157, 158, 201
Chávez, Hugo, 122
Chevènement, Jean-Pierre, 95–96

Chiapas (Mexico), 43–44, 108, 203, 232
Chomsky, Noam, 50, 119, 170, 243
Clarke, Tony, 60
Clinton, Bill, 41, 63
Colombia, 108, 130, 134, 170, 185, 190, 197, 225
Communist Refoundation Party (Italy), 74
Confederation Paysanne, 61
Continental Social Alliance, 51, 81, 84, 91, 97, 217, 232
Council of Canadians, 60
CUT (Workers' Central Union–Brazil), 62, 79, 84, 217

D

Davos (Switzerland), 52, 65, 66, 77–78, 85–87, 96, 104, 108, 111, 117, 122, 131, 165, 168, 170–72, 176, 178, 181–82, 234, 239. *See also* World Economic Forum
de la Cueva, Hector, 97
Debord, Guy, 48, 242
Direct Action Network, 57
Disobbedienti, 48
Doha (Qatar), 60, 65, 192, 238
Durão, Jorge, 84
Dutra, Olívio, 79, 92, 95

E

Earth Island Institute, 59
ECO-92 (1992 Earth Summit), 29, 47
Ecuador, 122, 136, 195, 216, 234, 240
Enron, 104, 189

European Social Forum (ESF), 120, 126–28, 135–36, 155, 158, 161, 240
European Union (EU), 16, 33, 42–43, 59, 62, 64, 67, 69, 121, 127, 142, 194–95, 237, 239

F

50 Years is Enough!, 67, 84, 97, 166, 209
Fiori, José Luis, 25
Fisher, William F., 113, 243
Florence (Italy) 116, 121, 126, 145, 240
Focus on the Global South, 60, 67, 81, 84, 97, 175, 177, 219, 229, 255
Fourth Declaration of the Lacandon Jungle, 44
France, 32, 42, 51, 53, 66, 67, 71, 72, 74, 78, 80, 95, 97, 126, 135, 167, 195, 200, 212, 220, 228, 229, 235, 237, 242
French Peasants Confederation, 84, 89
Free Trade Area of the Americas (FTAA), 51, 53, 64, 68–69, 83–84, 91, 107, 109, 125, 130, 142, 161, 176–77, 184, 186, 193, 195, 198–99, 207, 232, 237, 239

G

G-7, 32–34, 47, 51, 52, 64, 66, 235
G-8, 16–17, 29, 32–34, 64–65, 69–70, 84, 97, 103, 105, 126, 233, 238
General Agreement on Tariffs and Trade (GATT), 29, 58, 71

Geneva (Switzerland), 51, 53, 56, 61, 66, 79, 81, 84, 233, 235
Genoa (Italy), 17, 55, 64, 65, 69, 103, 105, 126, 186, 190, 203, 238
Genoa Social Forum, 69, 97, 105
Genro, Tarso, 95
George, Susan, 50, 56, 60, 167, 242
Germany, 32, 42, 127, 135, 213, 227
Giuliani, Carlo, 70, 238
Greece, 43, 127, 135
Green Party (U.S.), 57
Greenspan, Alan, 50
Guevara, Che, 44
Guimarães, Samuel Pinheiro, 104
Gupta, Amit Sen, 156
Gutierrez, Lucio, 122

H

Hardt, Michael, 120
Harry, Debra, 61
Harvey, David, 46, 49, 241
Hascoët, Guy, 95
Hawken, Paul, 61
Hirst, Paul, 25
Hobsbawm, Eric, 22, 49, 241
Hormoku, Tetteh, 61
Houtart, François, 97, 242
Hyderabad (India), 128, 145, 240

I

International Labor Organization (ILO), 114, 184, 191
India, 120, 129–33, 145–50, 153, 155–56, 161, 202–203, 205, 219–220, 236, 240, 244, 259, 260–61
Indian Organizing Committee

(IOC), 133–35, 147, 153, 156–57
Indigenous Peoples Camp, 83, 91
Indigenous Peoples Coalition
    Against Biopiracy, 61
Institute for Agriculture and Trade
    Policy, 60
Institute for Food and Development Policy, 60
Institute for Policy Studies, 60
Intergalactika, 107
International Committee, 79, 97
International Council (IC), 13, 95,
    97–99, 102, 107, 111–12, 116,
    118, 121, 123–25, 130–35, 137,
    141–42, 145, 156, 161, 163–64,
    221, 242, 259
International Court of Justice, 30
International Forum on Globalization (IFG), 58, 60, 178, 222
International Meeting for Humanity and Against Neoliberalism,
    51
International Monetary Fund
    (IMF), 16, 26–29, 31, 41, 59,
    64–65, 67–68, 71, 93, 116, 166,
    172, 184, 186, 189, 195, 199, 207,
    209, 212, 235, 236, 239, 249
International Network of Social
    Movements, 137, 141, 142
International Society for Ecology
    and Culture, 60
Iraq, 18, 120, 128, 132, 152, 153,
    160, 191, 196, 197, 198, 203, 206,
    231, 240
Italian Organizing Committee, 126

J

Jameson, Fredric, 49, 241

Japan, 30, 32, 33, 34, 66, 152, 235
Jobs with Justice, 66, 134, 222
Jubilee 2000, 51, 67, 233
Jubilee South, 84, 97, 113, 125, 222

K

Keene, Beverly, 97
Khor, Martin, 60
Klein, Naomi, 50, 96, 122, 165, 242,
    243, 250
Korten, David, 60
Kyoto Protocol, 29, 68

L

Landless Peasants Movement,
    169, 173
Latin American Council of Social
    Sciences, 81, 215
Latin American Information
    Agency (ALAI), 81, 211
Le Monde Diplomatique, 50, 53, 75,
    78, 81, 86, 167, 249
Löwy, Michael, 43, 85, 86
Lula, Luiz Inácio, da Silva, 95, 122,
    169
Luxemburg, 42

M

Maastricht Treaty, 42
Multilateral Agreement on Investment (MAI), 50–53, 66, 80, 232,
    233, 235
Mali, 125
Mander, Jerry, 60
Marcos, Sub-commander, 45
Marx, Karl, 30

McDonald's, 34, 47, 66, 87, 169
Mediterranean Social Forum, 136
Mercosur, 29, 90, 214
Mexico, 42, 43, 45, 48, 60, 68, 107, 170, 186, 194, 199, 215, 224, 232, 239
Mexico City (Mexico), 48, 179
Miami, Florida, 134, 135, 136, 199
Millennium Round, 56, 60, 61–63, 234
Mittal, Anuradha, 60
Monbiot, George, 50
Monsanto, 47, 87, 89
Morales, Evo, 122, 125
Morocco, 136
Movement for the Survival of the Ogoni People, 61
MST, 79, 83, 84, 85, 89, 223
Mumbai (India), 120, 133, 134, 136, 145, 146, 147, 148, 149, 150, 152, 153, 154, 155, 156, 157, 158, 159, 160, 161, 162, 203

N

Nader, Ralph, 57, 74, 226
North American Free Trade Agreement (NAFTA), 29, 42, 43, 45, 207
Naples (Italy), 32, 69, 136, 237
National Autonomous University of Mexico (UNAM), 48
Negri, Antonio, 50, 120, 243
Nepal (Bangladesh), 129
Netherlands, 42, 68
New Delhi (India), 147, 148, 244, 253, 254
New York, 53, 65–66, 108, 134, 149, 239

nongovernmental organizations (NGOs), 47, 49, 53, 66, 80, 81, 84, 94, 97, 109, 146, 154, 163, 166, 176–78, 181, 209, 216, 218, 225, 227
Nike, 47, 216
Njehu, Njoki Njoroge, 97
Norberg-Hodge, Helena, 60

O

Okinawa (Japan), 34, 66, 235
Organization for Economic Co-operation and Development (OECD), 23, 51, 52, 64, 71, 212, 233, 235
Organizing Committees, 98, 137, 141, 142, 163, 164
Ottawa (Canada), 53, 65

P

Palestine, 108, 117, 128, 152, 210, 239, 240
Pan-Amazon Forum, 136, 238
Paris (France), 51, 53, 128, 135, 145, 179, 233, 234
Parliamentarians Forum, 89, 159
People-Centered Development Forum, 60
Peoples' Global Action, 51
Peoples' Summit of the Americas, 51, 233
Philippines, 152, 219
piqueteros, 48
Plan Colombia, 130, 170, 185, 190
Polaris Institute, 60
Ponniah, Thomas, 112, 113, 243
Pontifical Catholic University,

(PUC), 82, 95, 117–19, 154
PSTU (United Socialist Workers' Party), 176
Public Citizen, 53, 57, 60, 170, 226
Puerto Rico, 32, 205, 236

Q

Quebec City (Canada), 68, 168, 186
Quito (Ecuador), 136, 195, 240

R

Raghavan, Chakravarthi, 61
Ramonet, Ignacio, 70, 71, 242
Reagan, Ronald, 16, 24, 231
Reclaim the Streets, 48, 53
Republican Party National Convention, 134
Rio Grande do Sul (Brazil), 79, 82, 83, 85, 91, 92, 109, 119, 121, 166
Rio+10 Conference, 108, 195
Ritchie, Mark, 60
Roque, Atila, 168, 172
Rousset, Pierre, 153
Roy, Arundhati, 119, 162, 243
Ruckus Society, 57
Russia, 32, 50
Russian Revolution, 24

S

San Francisco (U.S.), 53, 58, 216
Santos, Milton, 16, 247
São Paulo (Brazil), 13, 19, 78, 90, 97, 101, 140, 148, 178, 244, 245, 247, 249, 250, 252, 253
Seattle (U.S.), 17, 21, 23, 25, 27, 29, 31, 33, 35, 37, 39, 41, 43, 45, 47, 49, 51–72, 77, 80, 111, 137, 166, 167, 171, 182, 203, 216, 234, 242, 250, 251
Second World War, 22, 24, 26, 58
Sefarti, Claude, 120, 242
Seoane, José, 61, 62, 242
Seoul (Korea), 48
September 11, 2001, attacks, 17, 65, 74, 103–104, 120, 147, 188, 236, 238, 242, 251
Shiv Sena (Shivaji Army), 150
Shiva, Vandana, 60, 242
Social Forum of the Americas, 136
Social Movements International Secretariat, 68, 84
Social Watch, 97, 226, 228
South Africa, 24, 54, 195, 210, 222, 234, 238, 249
South Korea, 24, 45, 83
Soviet Union, 15, 22, 23, 24, 25, 32, 39, 49, 231
Spain, 108, 127, 136, 194, 195, 232, 239, 257
St. Clair, Jeffrey, 59
Stalinism, 159
Stedile, João Pedro, 87
Suplicy, Marta, 95
Sweeney, John, 45, 57, 170

T

Taddei, Emilio, 61, 62, 242
Thatcher, Margaret, 16, 24, 41, 111, 231
Thematic Social Forum, 128, 133, 239, 240
Thessalonia (Greece), 135
Third World Network, 60, 61, 227
Thompson, Grahame, 25

Tibet, 152
Tobin tax, 52, 89, 93, 113, 167, 193
Tobin, James, 167
Toussaint, Eric, 97, 242
Transnational Institute, 60, 227
TRIPS agreement (trade-related aspects of international property rights), 41
Tutte Bianchi, 48

U

U.S. Social Forum, 134
United Kingdom, 16, 32, 34, 41, 51, 74, 132, 206, 220, 233, 245–46

V

Venezuela, 122, 136, 197, 206
Via Campesina, 81, 84, 108, 115, 161, 228, 236, 242

W

Wainwright, Hilary, 173
Wallach, Lori, 53, 57, 60, 170
Washington, D.C., 53, 65, 68, 186, 199, 235, 239
Whitaker, Francisco, 77
Wiwa, Owens, 60
Workers' Party, Brazil (PT), 82, 85, 92, 110, 119, 158, 166, 251, 215
World Bank, 16, 26, 29–31, 41, 47, 59, 64–65, 67–69, 71, 93, 111, 116, 166, 184, 186, 195, 207, 209, 212, 236, 237, 245, 249
World Economic Forum, 52, 64, 66, 68, 77, 85, 96, 122, 124, 165, 171, 178, 182, 186, 234, 236, 239. *See also* Davos
World Forum for Alternatives, 81, 97, 229
World March of Women, 65, 84, 229, 235–36
World Parliamentary Forum, 82, 102, 110, 119
World Trade Organization (WTO), 16, 17, 26, 29, 41, 42, 51–53, 55, 56–63, 65, 93, 107, 113, 116, 142, 160, 166, 168, 172, 176, 177, 184, 192, 195, 198, 199, 202, 203, 207, 208, 212, 228, 233, 234, 238, 249
WSF Secretariat, 19, 68, 84, 118, 124, 132, 135, 137, 141, 142, 163, 223

Y

Youth Camp, 83, 89, 90, 105, 107, 117, 128, 135, 146, 155, 259

Z

Zapata, Emiliano, 44, 45
Zapatista Army of National Liberation (EZLN), 43, 45, 232, 242, 245
Zapatistas, 16, 44, 50, 172
ZNet, 119
Zurich (Switzerland), 52, 234

Also from Haymarket Books

WHAT'S MY NAME, FOOL? SPORTS AND RESISTANCE IN THE UNITED STATES
Dave Zirin　　　1 931859 20 5　　　July 2005

Edgeofsports.com sportswriter Dave Zirin provdes a no-holds-barred commentary on the personalities and politics of American sports.

"Zirin is America's best sportswriter."—Lee Ballinger, *Rock and Rap Confidential*

THE DISPOSSESSED: CHRONICLES OF THE DESTERRADOS OF COLOMBIA
Alfredo Molano　　　1 931859 17 5　　　April 2005

The fight for women's liberation is urgent—and must be linked to winning broader social change.

WOMEN AND SOCIALISM: ESSAYS ON WOMEN'S LIBERATION
Sharon Smith　　　1 931859 11 6　　　May 2005

The fight for women's liberation is urgent—and must be linked to winning broader social change.

A PEOPLE'S HISTORY OF IRAQ: THE IRAQI COMMUNIST PARTY, WORKERS' MOVEMENTS, AND THE LEFT 1924–2004
Ilario Salucci　　　1 931859 14 0　　　April 2005

The inside story of how the worldwide movement against corporate globalization has become such a force.

YOUR MONEY OR YOUR LIFE (3rd edition)
Eric Toussaint　　　1 931859 18 3　　　June 2005

Globalization brings growth? Think again. Debt—engineered by the IMF and World Bank—sucks countries dry.

THE STRUGGLE FOR PALESTINE
Edited by Lance Selfa　　　ISBN 1931859000　　　2002

In this important new collection of essays, leading international solidarity activists offer insight into the ongoing struggle for Palestinian freedom and for justice in the Middle East.

About Haymarket Books

Haymarket Books is a non-profit, progressive book distributor and publisher, a project of the Center for Economic Research and Social Change.

We believe that activists need to take ideas, history and politics into the many struggles for social justice today. Learning the lessons of past victories, as well as defeats, can arm a new generation of fighters for a better world.

We take inspiration and courage from our namesakes, the Haymarket Martyrs, who gave their lives fighting for a better world. Their struggle for the eight-hour day in 1886, which gave us May Day, the international workers' holiday, reminds workers around the world that ordinary people can organize and struggle for their own liberation. These struggles continue today in every corner of the globe—struggles against oppression, exploitation, hunger and poverty.

It was August Spies, one of the Martyrs who was targeted for being an immigrant and an anarchist, who predicted the battles being fought to this day. "If you think that by hanging us you can stamp out the labor movement," Spies told the judge, "then hang us. Here you will tread upon a spark, but here, and there, and behind you, and in front of you, and everywhere, the flames will blaze up. It is a subterranean fire. You cannot put it out. The ground is on fire upon which you stand."

Visit our online bookstore at www.haymarketbooks.org.

We could not succeed in our publishing efforts without the generous financial support of our readers. Many people contribute to our project through the Haymarket Sustainers program, where donors receive free books in return for their monetary support. If you would like to be a part of this program, please contact us at info@haymarketbooks.org.